IS IT

Poetry

Mike Greenhough

Copyright © Mike Greenhough 2020. All rights reserved.
ISBN 978-1-71685-416-3

No part of this book may be reproduced in any form or by any electronic or mechanical means, including information storage and retrieval systems, without permission in writing from the publisher, except by a reviewer who may quote brief passages in a review.

mikegreenhoughwriting.co.uk

Cover Design and Illustrations: Rose Horridge
www.rosehorridgeart.co.uk

Warning – these pieces contain no savage indictments of society, and shed no light on the human predicament. I'm not really the savage type, and the human predicament has already been distressingly well illuminated by countless others.

Contents

Jumping the Gun	7
Not to mention Vivaldi	8
Voids	9
Signora Galilei	10
Lovelines	10
Footloose	11
Great Alexander	12
The Giacometti Divorce	12
Re-arrangement in Grey and Black	13
Artist's Retreat	13
Forbidden Fruit	14
Mounting Anxiety	15
PDSA	16
Homers	17
Good Fences	18
Baa codes	18
Haiku	19
Possession	20
Une Leçon Musicale	22
Heldentod	22
Tempo Perduto	23
Northern Exposure	23
La Vallée Blanche	24
Terminal Velocity	26
What Am I?	29
IT	30
Obverse	36
Pacification	37
Unaccustomed as we are	38
Plattenspiel	39
IS	40

One-Bar Blues	46
Ruminants of Music	46
Dim innuendo	47
Blas Ar Gymru	47
Many a Slip	48
Kitchen-Wasteland	48
Festspiel	49
Category Mistake	49
Haiku	50
Kneeology	52
Command Performance	55
Boarder Lines	55
Datsun Diaspora	56
The Grand Tour of J Alfred Prufrock	58
Games to be played . . .	62
The Limits of Integration	62
Pays de Gals	63
Lapse	63
Buridan's Bull	64
Curtains	64
Humoresque	65
Dyslexia Nervosa	66
Belated Advice to Marie Antoinette	67
Weathermancy	67
Frozen Assets	68
Hidden Dragon	68
LAST ORDERS	69
Never Again	70
Bookends	71
Acknowledgements	72

Jumping the Gun

On learning, much later, I'd been born a week too soon,
I felt rather pleased.
Being early for your birth seems like simple good manners.
As noteworthy, perhaps, as being late for your own funeral,
But without the overtones of incompetence.

Did it confound the astrologentsia, thwart the auguries,
That, though intended for the Libras,
I balked at the zodiacal boundary
And landed in Virgo?
Just.
They say cusps like me share the characteristics of both,
Though in my, regretfully limited, experience,
Librarians and virgins form mutually exclusive groups.
So much for stereotyping.

Prematurity was no handicap at all,
I emerged as intact and functional as any full-termer.
A week is not a long time in obstetrics.
Indeed it gives you a bit of a start,
A sense of being somehow permanently ahead of the game,
Of having a lifelong edge on things.
I'm now content to read three-day-old newspapers,
And gleefully put second-class stamps on my letters,
Safe in the knowledge they will still get there
Days before they would have done
Had I been on time.

Not to mention Vivaldi

More than daffodils and lambs
or mellow fruitfulness,
more than sights and scents,
the seasons sing to us
our vital songs.
Without Summertime,
the livin' would not be easy,
the fish, lethargic,
the cotton, stunted.
No Winter, no wonderland;
and only Autumn can make
the leaves drift by my window.
But, most of all,
if they took away the Springtime
my fancy would have
nothing to turn to,
or you, my dear,
to be younger than.

Voids

After the fond farewell at Terminal Two,
the luxuries of space and time:
an hour of bathing, unmolested,
an acre of duvet, uncontested.
The note on the fridge I take at first
for a billet-doux,
or an ode to missing plums,
but all it says on closer inspection
is not to give the house plants too much water,
or too little –
the one deduction
(or is it two?)
I could have made
unaided.

Within a day the cat has learned the futility of looking for you,
high and low,
but won't share the secret.
I settle down to a regime of TV and takeaways.
Friday's neatly penned postcard triggers thoughts
of fond hellos,
and a frenzy of hoovering.
Twenty-four hours to contain myself
till you reappear and resolve all mysteries:
is the little red light on the boiler good news
or bad?
the languishing geranium parched,
or saturated?
Is *oregano* a colourless gas?
Or do we need to buy some more?

Signora Galilei

deeply dissatisfied,
nonetheless assures hubby
that the earth moved,
then swiftly recants,
sotto voce,
for the sake
of her immortal soul.

Lovelines

Madame Lissajous,
after months at the gymnasium,
attains the hourglass figure
that might keep Monsieur
from spending so long
at the laboratory.

Footloose

When televisual offerings are dire,
The evening paper read, the weather grim,
I draw an easy chair up to the fire,
And treat the ragged toenails to a trim.
The glinting clippers hover, swoop and shear;
Grey crescent moons of horny shrapnel fly,
To ricochet from clock or chandelier,
Then silent in the tufted Wilton lie.
Untimely ripped, do these poor souls lament
Their cheerless, disconnected destiny?
Or are such orphaned fragments well content
To savour one sweet hour of liberty
'twixt sock's removal and the dawn of light
And Hoover bag's entombing, endless night?

Η ζωή είναι σύντομη, η τέχνη μακρά

Great Alexander was a man apart,
At thirty years he'd conquered ev'ry land,
Built cities, mastered Poetry and Art,
And still had time to run a ragtime band.

† ars longa vita brevis (Hippocrates)

And some art is longa than other:

The Giacometti Divorce

That's mine!
No, *it's mine* ! ! !

No, *it's* mi i *i i i* i n n n e ! ! ! !

Re-arrangement in Grey and Black

After months of coaxing
with chocolates and cheesecake
Mother agrees to sit.
Whistling softly,
he prepares to paint
the landscape of a lady.

Artist's Retreat

Andrew Warhola,
after a hectic day at The Factory,
dismisses all aides and lackeys,
puts soup on to simmer,
then settles into the steaming bathtub
to savour his fifteen minutes of foam.

Forbidden Fruit: A Literature-Professor's Love Song

Ms V. Bramley-Cox, Ms V. Bramley-Cox,
With your soft plummy voice and luxuriant locks,
Demure on the front row through Shelley and Keats,
While my pulse palpitates and my heart overheats.

Smooth as an apricot, sweet as a pear,
Delicate, dainty, refined, debonair.
From the crown of your head to the toes of your socks,
Of blue-blooded family, my V. Bramley-Cox.

Am I courting disaster and risking the dole?
Have I over-extended my pastoral role?
Does it constitute gross dereliction of duty
To woo you, my extra-curricular cutie?

Fairest of creatures, temptress of teachers,
Ten out of ten for your peachy-cream features,
Cherry-lipped, apple-cheeked, golden, delicious,
Firm-fleshed and succulent, amply nutritious.

Victoria Cox, Ms Victoria Cox,
The face of an angel, the grace of a fox.
Let us away to a green forest glade,
Where a man can be man and a maid can be maid.

Ensconced in a love nest all comfy and cosy,
An hour of Persuasion, then Cider With Rosie.
What metrical magic together we'll weave
In our scholarly Eden – me Adam, you Eve.

Oh promise you'll be, my fruity tutee,
My delectable cocktail of vitamin C.
Hand in hand we'll meander through Byron and Brontë,
You Carmen Miranda, me Man from Del Monte.

Mounting Anxiety

Fräulein Maria reveals when she sings,
Only a *few* of her favourite things.
Is the tip of the iceberg all she admits?
Has she carefully censored the spicier bits?

Years of compliance and cloistered repression
Could lead a young novice to yearn for transgression.
We might well suspect that those items *un*listed
Are blasphemous, bawdy, immoral or twisted.

And noodles and Strudels and raindrops on roses
May signify more than at first one supposes.
What do you think Dr Freud and his cronies
Would make of those wild geese and cream-coloured ponies?

Kapitän von Trapp cannot wait to be told
Just what those brown paper packages hold.
And what's with the blue satin sashes and things?
Is it somebody's wish to be tied up with strings?

Well the wedding day dawns and the two tie the knot,
Then it's back to the Schloss to proceed with the plot.
Together at last with a bottle of Schnapps,
Having safely tucked in all those little von Trapps.

But what if so late in the day it emerges
The couple possess incompatible urges?
Will she turn out irredeemably chaste?
Or boldly unveil truly catholic taste?

So wish them good luck as these diffident souls
Prepare to enact their connubial roles.
Now hush, Julie Andrews is climbing the stairs,
And Christopher Plummer is saying his prayers.

PDSA

The animals came in one by one,
dragged or dragging, basketed, caged, shoeboxed,
or dangling unceremoniously underarm,
sporting poorly paws, mange, or noses judged too warm.

The receptionist, a volunteer, dark-smocked, love-labouring,
ticked them off,
repeating names of pet and owner,
like the guest list at an embassy ball,
or a running order of music-hall acts.
Mrs Fanthorpe and Foo Foo,
Barnaby and Mr Charles.
Then came Arnold and Wilberforce, who left us guessing
who was who.
Please take a seat, lap, floor.

No solemn silence here, like the doctor's or dentist's,
but a creeping crescendo as these furry catalysts
melted the ice between us.
Patch, limping, and the Smiths,
Eric and Tibbles.
Come on in, room for a little one, room for all.

Into this chorus of life manifold
was led one more,
slow, solid, unprotesting, sniffing its weary way
sans eyes and ears,
sitting straight down.
No names for the book, just a silent nod.
There was a hush in the jungle
as we clutched our darlings and stared down at the floor.

Homers

Five hundred miles
on a fistful of millet,
arrowing homeward,
following sun or stars,
lodestone or ley lines,
who can say?

In a recent documentary
fiendish avian psychologists,
seeking to pinpoint the trick of it,
appended a series of handicaps
and hindrances.

Off flapped the little chaps,
maplessly,
bearing frosted contact lenses,
nostril plugs,
magnets like millstones,
but no ill will, it seemed,
towards their tormentors,
whom they beat, repeatedly,
back to the loft.

You have to take your hat off to a creature
balloted so often on living conditions,
voting with its wings,
  YES,
                     YES,
                                  YES!

Put your spouse
in a wicker basket
on the night train to Huddersfield,
and you will scan
                        the horizon
        in vain.

Good Fences

Frostily they stare each other out
across the net I've stretched the garden long,
my neighbour and my cat,
two estimable creatures
separated by a common love of pigeons.

Baa codes

When a farmer dyes his sheep with coloured patches,
(so that in the round-up he will never miss 'em)
will their offspring sport a stain which closely matches,
or would that be tantamount to lamb-markism?

honk of south-bound geese
in the V's wake
the Doppler shock

duvet imprint
of a dawn-departed cat –
fossil ammonite

old tom cat
drapes the sun-baked garden wall
a watch by Dali

Possession

"I reckon they'll beat 'em," the barber begins,
"long as they keep possession."
In the mirror he jerks his head at the pre-match commentary
burbling in the background.

I grunt noncommittally.
Then add a nodding smile,
keen to conceal the true magnitude of my indifference
from a man with so many razors.

He snips and rants on –
wingers and flankers,
strikers and sweepers.
I smile and muse
on winners and keepers,
losers and weepers,
on what possesses a man to pursue with such covetousness
a harmless and inedible pound of leather.

I do remember dimly, but fondly,
a beach ball with bold, primary-coloured segments,
oversized, underinflated, and short-lived,
the victim of an ebbing tide.
Then the tennis ball, soggy and balding
which was shared, rather unequally, with next-door's spaniel.

But there would have been some first encounter,
with a football proper.
And it would have been decisive:

I close my eyes,
summon the swirling arpeggios;
the dreamy screen of memory
wavers, then clears to reveal
a small boy in the park.

I have fed the ducks and climbed an easy tree,
which now I sit against, watching the clouds go by.

Enter Boy Two: older, bigger, unthreatening.
He eyes me, moves the ball from toe to toe,
waggles his head side to side in a parallel gesture
which is clearly meant to be provocative,
though of what I am unsure.
"Come on!" He yells at last.
My frown intensifies.
"You've got to try and get the ball off me!"

And I remember thinking *no I haven't*
and wandering off towards the swings.

With swings you get one each.
I take my place on the shiny wooden seat,
grasp the cool metal chains,
dangle in uncontested luxury.

Sailing clouds, sighing trees,
distant contented quacks.

The snipping stops, I open my eyes
to rants and chants, cheers and jeers,
as somebody somewhere pursues somebody,
catches, beats, dispossesses,
only to be caught, beaten, dispossessed.

"That'll be seven pounds."
I brush the hair from my shoulders, depart,
think, how much serener life could be
if there were just twenty-two times as many footballs.

Une Leçon Musicale

Six young French composers
On the river bank –
Milhaud felt a sudden shove
Then there were cinq . . .

**The student is required to complete the piece
in a thematically and rhythmically consistent fashion**

Heldentod

A Wagner fanatic called Norma
Was obsessed with a leading performer;
She heard the man sing
Twenty times in *The Ring*
Then expired from post-operative trauma.

Tempo Perduto

Two Catholic fiddlers from Prato †
Got to practising more than vibrato;
They relied week to week
On the rhythm technique,
But alas, soon fell foul of rubato.

Northern Exposure

A compositor chappie from Crieff *
Wore a kilt that was frightfully brief;
In this state of undress
He leaned over the press
And went to his grave, sans serif.

† A city in Tuscany, population (in 2017) around 192,500 (and rising).

* A 'popular holiday resort' located within the unitary authority of Perth & Kinross, population (in 2017) around 7500 (and falling).

La Vallée Blanche – a haibun

We turn our backs on the highest cable car, which has delivered us to the glacier's edge, far above the tree line. In front of us, half a day's descent, powered only by gravity and a lunch-pack from the Chalet Belvedere.

Our guide, Claude, briefs the group: the weather is kind today – you can see three countries. But we must ski gently, breathe deeply, keep close behind. The glacier is unforgiving. Indifferent to human fate. Neolithic misadventurers emerge from time to time, way down in the valley. After the sleep of ice ages.

yawning crevasse
we contemplate
the longest way down

Faces are plastered with factor forty plus. Here is both Winter and Summer. Heart and breath find a new tempo, snow squeaks at higher pitch. A world transposed.

Claude is surprisingly stocky, reassuringly old, though the white in his beard is mainly frost. We zip every zip, follow him down. A motley crocodile. Another mountain's height above us a jet plane is Geneva bound. It leaves a silent curve clinging to the blueness. Don't look up!

I am the first to fall, silently. Harmlessly. Then up again and underway with a wide grin, before helping hands can reach. A virgin drift has been joyfully despoiled. The snow gods are placated, the group relieved. I have broken the metaphorical ice.

We pause every few minutes, catch our breath, before the view takes it away again. Claude counts heads – still eight – nods his own, tightens his bulky rucksack. I hope we won't need whatever is inside. "Allons-y!" he calls. We gaze at his exemplary tracks.

the master writes
followers
obscure the message

Claude steers us away from perilous edges, rocks, icy patches. Admonishes speeders. Our good shepherd. High-alpine gendarme.

We jockey for position in the group. I tuck in behind a young lady in stylish salopettes. Tight, fluorescent green. Ideal object of pursuit.

We take a late picnic lunch on the terrace of a refuge. Chocolate is traded for swigs of schnapps, old ski stories for more of the same. Comrades all, we move off again. Down, down. The sun is lost behind a ridge.

Down, down. Faces chill, thighs burn. Finally we join up with a normal piste. Our high-ground, rarefied heroism dissipates as we merge with hordes of the more timorous, on their last blue-run of the day. Into the village. We part with kisses, bear hugs. I head for Chalet Belvedere. It is our last night, fondue night, and I have a tale to tell.

Round the massive pine table the glow of candles. Faces. Vin rouge, high jinks. Past the windows, flakes begin drifting. Rumours of blizzards up high where I have been.

snow on snow
the day's adventure
put to bed

Terminal Velocity

Forget "*GERONIMO !*" !
That's for cowboys.
We count clearly
1000 2000 3000
and again
1000 2000 3000.

Not sure how long to pause between
 (are we *marching* or *waltzing* here?)
but am afraid to ask Instructor Norman, who's ex RAF.
Maybe it's not critical –
what's a crotchet rest between friends?
Well, about 80 feet, at the speed we'll be going.
That's the length of two London buses
(or four hearses, *de luxe* models).

Then when the counting's done, and not before, it's
CHECK CANOPY !
And you've got to look up and make sure it's untangled and intact,
full and round.
If so, you can float down in two to three minutes,
depending on your weight,
admiring the view.
If not, you have just a handful of heartbeats to deploy
the emergency 'chute.

In training Norman keeps shouting *You have a malfunction !*
He's only kidding, but you'll be grateful for the practice
if it really happens.
That's when you have to get it together, pull the toggle,
throw the thing outwards,
and sharp.

But you'll never have to. Really.

Norman urges us to handle the fabric.
It's silky, but very strong.
Feel the strength of it !
A good 'chute will last you twenty years, says Norman.
(True, maybe, but a bad one will last you a lifetime).

Over a light lunch I secretly, silently, rehearse.
1000 2000 3000, 1000 2000 3000, Check Canopy !
And look up at the ceiling.

Then it's off to the runway.

We sit in a line on the bench, like the dentists,
in intrepid quartets, nursing our toggles,
1000 2000 3000, 1000 2000 3000, Check Canopy !

We board the doorless Cessna
and climb in tight circles
around and around
1000 2000 3000, 1000 2000 3000, Check Canopy !

IN THE DOOR ! yells Norman, no messing.
I perch on the brink,
legs and heart adangle.
1000 2000 3000, 1000 2000 3000, Check Canopy !

Then it's **GO !**

                                                  I go,

Faaaaaaaking Heeeelll!

What am I?

The moving ballpoint writes and leaves behind
my blue-black patterns of alternate stress;
the strong succeeds the weak, as you will find,
and medium and message coalesce.
Self-reference is postmodernism's curse.
And I am what I am, ...

Answer: I am Bic verse!

IT: a celebration

To be read aloud, with discretionary bursting into song

It's a man's life,
it's a wonderful life,
it's a fine line,
it's a jungle out there,
it's a heartache,
it's a most unusual day,
a mad mad mad mad world,
a bonny bouncing boy,
it's an ill wind,
it's a sin, to tell, a lie.

It, as you see, is not unusual;
in fact, it's not just not unusual,
it's positively commonplace;
let's face it,
there's a lot
of it
about.
It's in the air,
it's everywhere,
and so, amenable:
you can make it, fake it,
move it, groove it,
vaunt it,
flaunt it, even,
assuming you've got it to begin with;
you can milk it, mix it,
get Jim to fix it,
darn it, damn it,
get Sam to play it again.

It: your flexible friend.

But what does it mean,
exactly?
Having brought it up,
can we pin it down, and find
the crux of it,
the nub of it,
the pith, the gist, the quintessential nitty gritty,
of it?

First, habitat.
It likes to hang out with prepositions:
you can set it off, set it up,
set it down, set it out,
turn it out, turn it in,
turn it off, turn it on,
turn it up, turn it down.
You can knock it off, block it off,
pack it in, jack it in,
break it in, rake it in.

It: the monosyllable with a thousand uses:

you can live it up, give it up,
set it up, get it up,
scoop it up, whoop it up,
or fight it out, write it out, sit it out, let it out
heave it out, leave it out, spit it out, sweat it out,
shut it out,
cut it out.

It: the Swiss army knife of the English language.

It, is the stuff of idiom:
the it you've never had so good!
the it that shouldn't happen
to a dog,
the it you have to like or lump,
lock or lose,
the it you shouldn't knock
until you've tried,
the it that's cold outside, baby;

the it you can watch for hours,
the it you can say with flowers.

A bouquet of its.

The urgent it:
that drives you to drink,
that's later than you think.

The paradoxical it:
if it's such a small world, how come it's still a long way
to Tipperary?
I think we should be told.

There's masses of its,
mountains of its,
we're up to our ears;
in its.

The it that's finger-lickin' good,
the it that couldn't happen,
to a nicer chap;
the it we're gonna have to face,
the it that came from outer space,
da da DAAAAA !

A galaxy of its.

The musical it:
that everybody's doing,
that's now or never,
foolish, but fun,
that's only just begun,
that had to be you,
makes my brown eyes blue
and takes two to tango;
the it that's not the pale moon,
that's too soon to know,
that's off to work we go.

Hi – Ho . . . ♫

Its for all occasions;
its for me;
it's for you-hoo!

The it that's all too much,
the it I wouldn't touch
with a barge pole,
the it we have to grin and bear,
the it that simply isn't fair,
the it you'd better hold right there,
Mister!

The it I remember well, ♫
the it that you can go tell
either on the mountain,
or to the marines,
depending on personal proclivities,
the it that some like hot,
that you believe, or not,
the it you've either got
or you haven't,
the it that I forbid,
the it the butler did,

allegedly,

the it that might as well be spring,
the it that just don't mean a thing
without that certain swing,
Do-wah do-wah do-wah do-wah do-wah do-wahhh . . .

The it that's a great big shame,
the it I'll play, if you name,
and that you can either blame on the bossa nova
or the boogie,
depending on your Terpsichorean tastes;
the it we shouldn't try to fight,
the it that's gonna be all right
on the night.

Oodles of its, lashings of its
a veritable blitz, of its.

The literary it:
it was a lover and his lass,
it was a dark and stormy night,
it was the best of times,
it is the east,
it is twice blest,
it is an ancient mariner,
and a far far better thing.
It is a consummation devoutly to be wished.
It, is a truth universally acknowledged.

It: the honest, unsung, worker-ant
of the pronoun kingdom.

The it that's early days,
that cuts both ways,
that pays to advertise,
the it the 'ayes' have.

The abstruse, convoluted it:
that it as luck would have,
that easy does,
with which what's love got to do,
that if anything can go wrong will;
the it away from all of which we might consider
getting.

And there we have it –
the multi-talented, many-splendoured it,
that 'S wonderful, that 'S marvellous
and not just delightful and delicious but deelovely,
into the bargain.

So many its, so little time,
you haven't heard the half of it,
just a brief report,
not the long and short of it.
But it's time to give it a rest,
to call it a day,
it's all over, my friend (eughh!!!),
it's the end,
it's a wrap,
the fat lady has sung.
So, cheer it or jeer it,
revile or revere it,
let's hear it
for IT!

Obverse

No wave without water,
no still-life without canvas,
no song without the unsung silence.
Spare a thought for
heroic supporting acts,
the also-rans who also serve.
I have a soft spot for Cinderellas –
you may think these are my printed words;
in truth I started with
a plain black page
and tippexed out the bits
that didn't look like a poem.
Though I may have missed a few.

Pacification

     from the
Caribbean coast
 across the wastes of Venezuela
  down, down, through forests
of Amazon the panpipes call us, following the
condor's flight, into Peru, along the Andes,
lake and torrent, valley and pampas grass,
   down, down, till this land, narrowing now
     in the grip of Atlantic and Pacific, nears
        the tongue tip of Tierra del Fuego,
          and the cauldron of Cape Horn
           seals the fate of a hundred
           ships, ten thousand souls,
           victims in a ceaseless
          war of two mighty
         oceans. You would
        think someone
      would have had
      the wit
      to re-
     name
     one
      of
      them.

Unaccustomed as we are

The
smartly
dressed man
raps on the
table with a
salt pot and,
forgetting for
a moment that
we are not at a
wedding reception,
we fellow diners fall
silent, fixing our gaze
on him politely and
expectantly as he
sprinkles his chips.

Ernst Florens Friedrich Chladni
gently taps the plate of cake crumbs

ponders the resulting pattern
licks away the nodal lines.

𝔓lattenspiel

IS

Performance directions: see **IT** *!*

We begin with some is statistics:
if all of the *is*es that all of us use in a year
were typed end to end,
they'd stretch to the sun!
(At least in Times New Roman, 12-point font).
It could be the *was*es would reach just as far
but only because was is longer than is.
We do in fact use more ises than wases,
and it seems we're living for the moment,
because the *will be*s would barely make it to the moon.
As for the has beens,
they've had their day.

Which brings us to the history of is.

In the beginning was is;
now the world is everything that is the case,
and everything that is, is, something, or other;
if nothing else, it's itself:

A rose is a rose,
a spade, a spade,
a deal a deal,
rules, rules;
business is business,
east east,
west west,
war war,
the law, the law.
This is is the is of truism.

There are other ises:
this, is the moment,
that, the question,
love the answer,
there is more.

Lots more:
small is beautiful,
love, blind,
ignorance bliss,
history bunk.
And that's just some of the *B*s!

But a rose is still a rose,
a kiss, just a kiss,
a sigh a sigh.
Of all the verbs in all the world, the busiest is is.

Knowledge is power,
now, the hour,
tomorrow, another day.

This is the is of worldly wisdom:
revenge is sweet,
heat, work,
work heat,
meat murder,
fat a feminist issue;
duty's duty,
truth, beauty,
might is right,
tonight the night,
black is black,
Macky, back in town.

Is: the ever-popular copula.

Is is, as often as not, unspoken;
you've already heard this is,
or rather you haven't,
between the lines of this piece;
this is the is of ellipsis –
that is, that is that is lurking off-stage, but, implicitly, makes
the corn green,
the grass, greener,
the livin' easy,
the cotton high,
the sky the limit,
the night tender,
love, a many-splendoured thing.

Is: conspicuous by its absence;

Is: the missing mass that holds our world of words together;
which brings us to the science of is.

Theoretical poetical particle physicists at CERN reckon
that colliding a beam of high-speed *i*s
with a beam of oncoming *s* s
could create a shower of *is*es,
or, who knows, by reversing the field, a shower of *isn't*s.
They say, what's more, that if an is and an isn't were to meet
there'd be mutual annihilation
in a puff of pure ontological energy,
though sensitive detectors might just register
the presence of *wasn't*s.
Local literary critics warn
the resulting grammatical singularity
could swallow half of Switzerland.

Is: the vital little boson of our English prose.

Is is a word of many moods.

The exuberant is:
life is a boon,
the moon, a balloon,
June, bustin' out all over.

The mystical, biblical is:
the Lord's my Shepherd,
Moab, my washpot,
my brother Esau, an hairy man.

The inquisitive is:
is it a bird, is it a plane?
Is it art (or even poetry)?
Is it safe, to drink the water?
Is this a dagger?
Is that a gun?
Is there honey still for tea?

What is life?   Just a bowl of cherries.
Where is love?   Just around the corner.
Who is Sylvia?   What is she?
She, is the cat's mother.

A catechism of ises.

The slanderous is:
the gentleman's a dope,
the lady, a tramp,
Sharon a slag,
allegedly;
Gordon, a moron.

Fair is foul and foul is fair,
the air is humming
and sumer is icumen in.

Is: a whizz of a word that tells you what's what
and, what's more, what's where.

This is is the is of location;
the world is everything that is the case
and every single thing requires
a place to be;
that's why space is so big.

First there is the is of on:
the lark is on the wing,
the snail, the thorn,
the cat the mat,
the moose the loose,
the horse the hoof,
the fiddler the roof,
the man the ledge,
the audience the edge, of their seats.

The scotch is on the rocks,
the tide, the turn,
the TV the blink,
the world, the brink of disaster;
the writing's on the wall,
the rain the plain,
the moon the wane,
the word the street,
the boot, the other foot.

Everywhere you look, things,
on top of other things,
which's why you can never find stuff.

Then there is the is of in:
love is in the air,
the ball, your court,
my fate your hands,
your life their hands;
a place for everything and everything in its place;
the cheque's in the post,
the sheep, the meadow,
the cow the corn,
the cat the cupboard,
the man the moon,
the sting the tail,
the message the song,
the devil the detail,
God, his heaven,
your dinner, the oven.

Is: without it *where* would you be?
Indeed where, or what, would anything
be?
Would a rose be still a rose?
Would this list still be endless?

But enough is enough
and less is more,
time is short
and art is long;
the song is ended,
the rest, silence,
whereof one cannot speak.

Except, to raise a toast
to that talented little syllable,
the present-tense, third-person singular of to be,
that verbal virtuoso,
viz., IS.

One-Bar Blues

Had a lie-in this mornin'.

Doh
A
Deer

Ruminants of Music #1.

Dim innuendo

We struggle to erect
the music-stands
and deck-chairs
of life only
to find
the song
ended
and
the sun
about
to
set
•

WELSH. IN. THESE. SCONES
CAKES. RISE. THE. RAISINS
AND. ARIAS. RING. SING

Blas Ar Gymru

(After Gwyneth Lewis)

Literary Lunches

Many a Slip

Alexander Isayevich Solzhenitsyn,
unaccustomed to ladling stew,
soils the virgin table cloth
with a goulash archipelago.

Kitchen-Wasteland

Thomas Stearns Eliot,
besieged by stray cats,
is dismayed to find
the cupboard bare,
no feline fare.
*Oed' und leer
der Frigidaire.*

Festspiel

Terence Mervyn Rattigan,
aproned at the barbecue,
sips the White Riesling,
hums The Blue Danube,
bastes the browning Würstchen.

Scene II: Not A Sausage

Thomas Stearns Eliot,
last in the long line,
glumly returns to his seat,
not with a banger, but a wimpy.

Category Mistake

Gilbert Ryle,
startled by the smoke alarm,
scours the kitchen
for smouldering nub ends,
momentarily unmindful of
the toast in the machine.

showering to Brahms
ears are washed
one at a time

removed for winter
the hose leaves its signature
scrawled across the lawn

hand-waving diner
drowning in a forlorn state
of waitresslessness

clothes gone to good causes
the unshiftable wardrobe
reverberates

broken sunglasses
mended with sticking plaster
healing will be slow

naked, supine
feeling sunset's slanting rays
tangenitally

Kneeology

To begin in the mists of prehistory,
(as Alexander Pope might have had it):

All nature stands stiff-legged 'till God decrees,
"Mankind must learn to dance, let there be knees!"

And there *were* knees.

Now flies have knees and fleas have knees
And hairy chimpanzees have knees,
Birds have knees and bees have knees
(the bees' being, of course, the best).

There's left knees, right knees,
black knees, white knees,
knees indeed of every creed, and nation:

Slavonic knees, Teutonic knees,
Angelic and demonic knees,
Conventional and quirkish knees,
Albanian and Turkish knees.

Strong knees, weak knees,
Grenadian and Greek knees,
Slav knees, suave knees,
Chic knees, and meek knees:

The humble nun has pliant knees
to bend in fervent prayers,
The Nepalese have giant knees
to scale the Himalayas.
Beloved of both the nuns and Sherpas,
Knees – so neatly multipurpose:

The sporty French ride bikes with 'em,
The hearty German hikes with 'em,
The Dutch block leaky dykes with 'em,
Knees – your flexible friends:

Lowly perch for saints, or sinners,
Handy stand for TV dinners,
Nature's nimble, springy hinges,
Broad, or slim as Fred and Ginger's.

History abounds with notable knees:

Genghis Khan and Julius Caesar,
Marilyn Monroe, Mother Teresa –
every one possessed them.
Lord Nelson sported sunburnt knees,
befitting of a sailor;
Napoleon wore dungarees
and thus his knees were paler (and, of course, bony.)

So, wearing shorts, revealing knees
gives keys to our identities
('by their knees ye shall know them'):

Chimney sweeps' and miners' knees
are battered, bruised and grimy,
While Martian knees (which come in threes)
are little, green and slimy.

Knees obscure and knees renowned,
Knees to make the world go round,
Knees to make the heart grow fonder,
Knees to roam the wild blue yonder.

Knees of Cubans, Poles and Gurkhas,
fit for mambos and mazurkas,
fit for foxtrots and fandangos,
Highland Flings and torrid tangos.

So remember, never denigrate your knees –
these most universal of all joints:
the spice of life, the windows of the soul;
they can move mountains,
or launch a thousand ships.

Whether noble or plebeian, Kuwaiti or Korean,
Grecian, Venetian, Tahitian or Fijian,
Russian, Prussian, Chinese or Thai knees,
These are the *Knees of the World* –
All human life is there!

Command Performance

Private Perkins, newly recruited,
enjoys an energetic game of footy
in the mud of no-man's-land,
shares crumpled photos,
Schnapps and Christmas Pud
with his new friend, Fritz,
before abruptly terminating festivities
with an injudiciously loud rendering of
Chestnuts Roasting on an
Open Fire.

Boarder Lines

A budding surf rider from Borth,
Craving challenging waves, travelled North;
He found more around Perth,
Than the land of his birth,
And no dearth in the Firth of the Forth.

Datsun Diaspora: an auto-biography

Riding along in my automobile,
lacking distractions of passengers or radio,
headlights on an empty road ahead
invite reflection –
on life and death, flesh and blood,
on the sparks and friction which keep us going,
and wear us out.

We scraped through the MOT this year,
with a lick of paint, a spot of welding,
a measure of luck.
And though assured "there's a good few miles in it yet"
I envisage journey's end for my trusty, rusty Nissan,
my ailing, failing, Sunny boy.

The metal skeleton is first to perish,
compacted to a cuboid,
then fused with fellow wrecks in a fiery smeltdown,
recast, reborn, transported, incorporated
in a bridge, girder, pylon, gantry.

In a reversal of nature, it is the soft parts that endure.
The back seat, shiny with secret histories,
is plucked out by the scrapyard owner,
to lean against his caravan, facing south,
where he sits for years with an old dog and a mug of tea.

The tyres will see more of the world:
the worn-out spare goes straight on the bonfire
and avenges itself by besmirching the washing
for miles around.

The two front cross-plies are rolled down a gravelly beach
by local urchins,
taken by the tide and borne away towards the Sargasso sea,
but rescued en route and pressed into service
as dockside fenders,
tethered alongside their cousins from Michelin, Dunlop, Goodyear.

The rear radials, having a little life in them yet,
are exported more formally,
to a region with laxer laws on depth of tread,
giving years of service on a tropical taxi,
squashing already squashed fruit in the market streets.
Then, in a third and final incarnation,
they hang from ropes in the local zoo,
providing diversion and exercise to a family of bonobos.

So much to offer
in going the way of all matter and metal.
Destiny calls to man and machine;
we can but delay.
Tomorrow, I'll book a full service, join a gym,
monitor more vigilantly the pressure of blood and tyres,
fill in the organ-donor card.
Meanwhile, eyes to the front, foot to the floor,
full beam ahead,
soul to soul, soft parts to soft parts,
we rattle along.

The Grand Tour of J Alfred Prufrock

Il mangiare non è mai finito, solo abbandonato

I

April, Sunday, *Galleria degli Uffizi, Firenze*

Can barely see the Michelangelos,
over the heads of all these women,
walking, talking, pushing and shoving;
coming and going.
Just as well they stuck his *David* on a plinth.

To narrow backstreet trattoria I retreat,
To face defeat by heap of pale spaghetti:
Dull, endless, like a tedious argument.
Where is there an end of it? Or beginning?
I little doubt this glutinous excess
Contributes to my later sleeplessness.
I read much of the night,
Then go south.

From artful exploration I'll not cease:
Munch, Michelangelo, Manet, Matisse . . .

II

Tuesday, *Capella Sistina*

Can barely see *The Last Judgment*
for the legions of women,
coming and going.
Just as well they let him paint on the ceiling too.

Repair to cheap and cheerless pizzeria,
To chew upon another doughy disc.

I grow weary.
I grow weary of this circumscribed cuisine:
Pizza, pasta,
Basta! Basta!

But when in Rome . . .

Round the turning world I go
Pastures new, Westward Ho !

III

May, Monday morning, Baltimore, Maryland

Can't face Art on an empty stomach,
and head for the harbour,
where clam chowder proves a fine starter,
but the crab-meat tastes funny;
I eat, one single claw,
then scuttle back to bed,
ragged, rotten,
Art, forgotten,
stomach, empty once more.

One must be so careful these days.
To everything there is a season:
a time for crustaceans (and regurgitations),
a time for taking of a toast and tea.

Oh keep the crab far hence, no friend to men,
'till months contain the letter 'r' again.

IV

June, Rio de Janeiro, Brazil

Restless night alone in cheap hotel.

Note: must insist on decaff coffee,
and smaller spoons.

At Ipanema I walk upon the beach.
The local girls they come and go:
Young and lovely, tall and tanned,
But they do not sing to me –
My rolled-up trouser bottoms full of sand,
My sunburnt bald patch there for all to see.

Note: must buy shorts,
and high-factor *Ambre Solaire*.

Round and round the globe I trot,
White flannel trousers, pink bald spot.

Thus blithely, from high church to low canteen,
I drink my fill of culture and cuisine,
with dishes more exotic with each visit,
and rarely do I dare to ask, What is it?

for, when in Rome . . .

V

July, South Korea,

(after a jug and a half of rice wine)

And is this, after all, my final goal –
This sordid, sawdust restaurant in Seoul?
I'm facing now an overwhelming question,
Concerning foreign food and its ingestion.
Have I, through these unsavoury excursions,
Conquered all gastronomical aversions?
Befogged, nay, *etherized*, by local hooch,
Do I dare? Do I dare to eat a pooch?

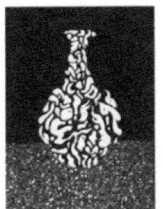

Games to be played when nobody comes to your party

Musical Chair,
Hold the Parcel,
Sardine,

Suicide in the Dark.

∫ **The Limits Of Integration**

After the party
I pack tomorrow's lunchbox with leftover biscuits:
Choco Leibniz, Fig Newtons.
In the night, muffled, fragmentary disputation.
In the morning, just crumbs.
Countless.
Infinitesimal.

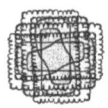

Pays de Gals

A visiting roué from Cannes
Had mixed luck as a Welsh-ladies' man;
He said "Gwenny and Gaynor
Could not have been plainer,
Mais je ne regrette Rhian."

Lapse

An archbishop, long past his youth,
Denied having wooed Rabbi Ruth;
Still, the look on his face
Said His Grace was a trace
Ecumenical, here, with the truth.

Buridan's Bull

A bull had a cow-friend called Emma,
Whose bovine twin sister was Gemma;
Since he couldn't decide
Which to take as his bride
Life was just one long horny dilemma.

Curtains

Yevgeny Nesterenko,
renowned Russian bass,
nurses the sumptuous bouquet
and bows to thunderous applause,
unaware that
during the final Act of Prince Igor,
due to a typographical error at the Pentagon,
his co-ordinates have been loaded
into the guidance system
of a Pershing II missile.

Humoresque

As the maestro
flips his coat-tails
over the back
of the piano stool
I insinuate
a packet
of cheesy snacks
and retire
to savour
the sound
of
hemidemisemiquavers.

Dyslexia Nervosa

It's the words,
the *words*,
they won't leave me alone.
Day and night
they flit and dance,
swarming, merging, blurring
in my peripheral vision
as I make the morning coffee,
boring into the back of my head
when I'm washing up.
And if I sneak down for a midnight snack
they confront me,
gang up in phrases,
switch places,
admonishing, accusing, confusing.
I beg the doc to tell me what it means,
but he says they are all just
magnets of my refrigeration.

Belated Advice to Marie Antoinette

There is often a statistical solution
To those problems that might threaten revolution.
There's no need to lose your head
When told the peasants have no bread,
Simply organise a croissant distribution.

Weathermancy

Michael John Fish,
in from the sudden shower,
draws a fine-tooth comb
through thinning locks
and holds it to the sky to see
a glistening histogram of rainfall.

Frozen Assets

If disparaged by proud Esquimaux
For having so few words for snow
Just concede, don't be miffed,
Keep it cool, get my drift?
Show you know how to go with the floe.

Hidden Dragon

A plucky conductor from Blaina
Was waylaid by the triads in China.
With a flick of her stick
And a quick kung-fu kick
She reduced them from major to minor.

LAST ORDERS

ALL PATRONS WE RESPECTFULLY INVITE
TO EXERCISE RESTRAINT AT CLOSE OF DAY
AND KEEP THE NOISE DOWN AS YOU LEAVE THIS SITE.

BE SYMPATHETIC TO OUR NEIGHBOURS' PLIGHT;
THEY LOOK ON CLOSING TIME WITH MUCH DISMAY.
SOME POOR SOULS HAVE TO GET UP AT FIRST LIGHT.

WILD MEN WHO DRINK THEIR FILL ARE NOT POLITE –
INSTEAD OF HEADING HOME WITHOUT DELAY
THEY HANG AROUND TO SING OR SWEAR AND FIGHT.

SOME SLAM THE COUPÉ DOOR WITH ALL THEIR MIGHT,
THEN REV THE ENGINE AS THEY PULL AWAY,
AND SCREECH THEIR SPORTY TYRES, JUST OUT OF SPITE.

THE LOCAL BOROUGH COUNCIL HAVE THE RIGHT
TO TERMINATE OUR LICENCE, AND THEY MAY,
IF ALL THOSE RAGING RESIDENTS UNITE.

SO OFF YOU TODDLE, HOMEWARD, AND SLEEP TIGHT –
NO BRAWLING, CATERWAULING ON THE WAY.
TO SUM UP, AT THE RISK OF SOUNDING TRITE:
PLEASE, DO GO GENTLE INTO THAT GOOD NIGHT.

Never Again

In this state
it's fifty-fifty
I'd get out of bed the wrong side,
but the undeniable plaster wall tips the odds in my favour;
the slippers, though, do end up on the wrong feet.
Still, they're my slippers,
and my feet
and two out of three isn't bad,
considering.
It's also my pain and my head,
my taste and my mouth,
however much I will a dissociation.
Coffee calls.
The stairs are innumerable,
even downhill,
and one at a time.
I disrupt a cairn of mail on the hall mat,
pass the mirror, eyes averted,
open the blind on ambiguous weather.
I confront the wall clock,
rap absently on the glass with finger tips.
The trembling second hand lurches forward.
I've said it before and I'll say it again –
it's going to get later.
You just mark my words.

Bookends

A fleeting glance
across a crowded branch
of Waterstones.
Discretely distant
I follow you
into Poetry, where,
consistent with priorities of arrival,
you begin to work your way
left to right,
top to bottom,
from Auden onwards,
while I make a beeline for Yeats.
Lingering over Virgil
I trust you will infer pastoral contemplation
and not, in your tight and daring denim,
misconstrue my recumbent posture.
And shelf by shelf your literary high ground
is conceded to mine,
in closing, browsing zigzags.
The alphabet dictates
accelerating heart rates,
the shop holds its breath
as we speed respectively
through Larkin and Plath.
Then, the meeting of minds, eyes, hands,
in a final, compromising grab
for Roger McGough.
And we hear the cheers
from Art
to Zoology.

Acknowledgements

Some of the pieces in this collection have found favour in competitions and/or been published or broadcast.

Kneeology – winner of the Percy French Award for Comic Verse after a performance at the Strokestown International Poetry Festival, Ireland, 2017.

Mounting Anxiety – 1st prize in Caerleon Festival All Wales Comic Verse Competition, 2012, and broadcast on Radio Wales.

removed for winter and *hand-waving diner*, were published in **Presence** haiku magazine.
La Vallée Blanche (haibun); *old tom cat*; *showering to Brahms*; *duvet imprint* and *honk of south-bound geese* (haiku) were all prize winners in the Annual Winchester Writers' Conference haiku competitions (sponsored by the British Haiku Society) (as was *clothes gone to good causes*) and were published in the conference anthologies, *The Best of 2002; 2007; 2009* and *2012*.

Forbidden Fruit – winner of the 'Adult Internet' (!) category of Ottakar's and Faber National Poetry Competition, and published in *Roundyhouse* magazine. *Bookends* was runner up in *The New Writer* Poetry Competition, and published in *The New Writer* magazine. Along with *PDSA*, these two also were prize winners in competitions sponsored by the Southern Daily Echo.

Homers – 1st prize in poetry competition, 2011;
Lapse and *Boarder Lines* – 1st prizes in limerick competitions, 2011 & 2018, all at Abergavenny Eisteddfod.

Diminuendo; *Humoresque*; *Games to be played when nobody comes to your party* and *What am I?* were all winners in the Fish Micro-Fiction Competitions and published in the Fish Anthologies of 2008 and 2009.

What Am I? was broadcast on BBC Radio Three's *The Verb* in 2007.

Frozen Assets – 1st prize in the Writers Bureau competition, 2015, published in Freelance Market News.

Jumping the Gun – 3rd prize in the *Rhyme and Reason* competition, 2011. Published, as were *Not to mention Vivaldi*; *Obverse* and *Festspiel*, in the *Rhyme and Reason* Desk Diaries of 2012; 2013 and 2016.

I gratefully acknowledge the above competition sponsors and the inspiration of John Betjeman (*Forbidden Fruit*), Dylan Thomas (*Last Orders*) and Rodgers and Hammerstein (*Mounting Anxiety*).

For many years Mike Greenhough lectured and researched in physics and the science of music at Cardiff University. He has long had a little toe in the arts, and has served on the judging panel for *sciart* awards – funding for collaborations between established writers, musicians and visual artists, and scientists. He has numerous awards for comic poems and short stories, winning the inaugural All Wales Comic Verse Competition, the Percy French Award for Comic Verse and a Canongate Prize for New Writing. This is his first poetry collection. His first novel, *Malcolm: Volume Zero*, is available from **Lulu.com**. Mike sails and skis.

mikegreenhoughwriting.co.uk

L - #0324 - 060720 - C0 - 210/148/4 - PB - DID2864187

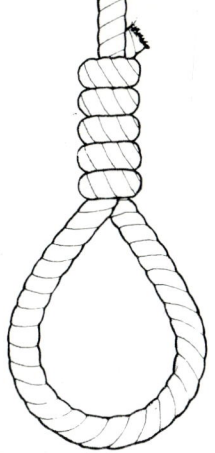

May the Lord have Mercy on Your Soul

MURDER AND SERIOUS CRIME IN DERBYSHIRE
1732 – 1882

Philip Taylor

© 1989

Series Editor: Peter J. Naylor

ISBN 0 946404 81 X

Printed and Published by
J. H. Hall & Sons Limited, Siddals Road, Derby
Printers and Stationers since 1831
Telephone: Derby (0332) 45218

THE DERBYSHIRE HERITAGE SERIES

*"Calm and composed my soul a journey takes,
no guilt that troubles, nor a heart that aches".*

PREFACE

This book tells the story of the Derbyshire men, and women, who received the death sentence for their terrible — and sometimes not so terrible — crimes during the one hundred and fifty year period 1732 - 1882.

The reason for terminating the book at this date was not arbitrary. Inevitably, a book of this nature could evoke unhappy memories for those people who were caught up in such tragic events. This is particularly true if the event is of comparatively recent origin, and is still fresh in the minds of relatives and friends of those involved

With this thought in mind, the editor and myself have decided to exclude any case less than a hundred years old, in order to protect the feelings of those who must otherwise be caused pain and embarassment.

Many of the younger readers of this book will be unfamiliar with pre-decimal coinage, so I have provided the new monetary values in parenthesis to assist them in understanding. Wherever possible, however, I have preferred to adopt the contemporary terminology, because this adds to the historical feel of the period. It would seem inappropriate, for example, to speak of a highwayman relieving a traveller of £2.10p, rather than two guineas.

During the eighteenth, and early nineteenth centuries, the capital penalty was employed so frequently that it has been impossible to touch on every case that merited the sentence. I have, therefore, confined myself to a study of those criminals who were actually executed for their misdeeds.

The restrictions of the death penalty to murder in the early Victorian period has enabled me to study the subject in greater detail.

Primary sources relating to the eighteenth century are scarce, so I have had to rely for most of my information about this period from volumes of the Derby Mercury which date from 1732.

The Victorian period, however, is more thoroughly documented.

The newspapers of the period are a rich source of information, invariably carrying comprehensive, and sometimes verbatim, accounts of the murder trials and the last letters and confessions of the condemned men prior to their execution.

ACKNOWLEDGEMENTS

I am indebted to Miss Sylvia Bown, Jaqui Sheppard, and all the staff of the Local Studies department of Derby Central Library, who responded patiently, and cheerfully to my incessant requests for nineteenth century newspapers and pamphlets.

Finally, I would like to extend my gratitude to my brother, Patrick Taylor, who spent many long hours typing the manuscript for this book.

Chapter I

GEORGIAN CRIME

During the last half of the eighteenth century Britain experienced a population explosion.

The local authorities of the country struggled to cope with problems raised by this explosion. The forces of law and order, in particular, were stretched to their limits. This was especially important for the eighteenth century was a very violent age.

Throughout the eighteenth century, and well into the nineteenth, riots were common, and these could assume frightening proportions. The anti-Catholic Gordon riots in 1780, for example, resulted in 700 deaths, and the destruction of property in London ten times that suffered by the Parisians in the French Revolution.

Some riots had their origins in social injustices. The crowds frequently attacked institutions they considered unjust, or defended customs they had come to regard as their rights.

Food riots were common. In times of shortage, millers would often resort to flour hoarding and over-pricing. The crowds retaliated by physically preventing millers and farmers selling their goods above a fixed price. In effect they imposed a 'moral economy' on the producers of food.

Derbyshire was by no means immune from these disturbances. There were particularly bitter bread riots in Derby in 1740 and 1756, which resulted in serious injuries to the people involved.

Riots of this kind disappeared later in the century due to a sustained increase in agricultural production, but civil disorders arising from other causes posed serious problems for the authorities well into the following century.

Derby experienced serious riots after the House of Lords rejected the First Reform Bill in 1831 for example, and as late as 1846 troops had to be used to restore order and protect property after a particularly robust game of Derby football.

In towns like Derby militia were often stationed to prevent such disorders. They were generally effective in quelling collective law breaking but they were totally inappropriate for the everyday policing required to protect citizens from the depredations of conventional criminals, tenaciously pursuing a philosophy of individual self-help.

Eighteenth century Britain was far from crime-free. This was the golden age of the highwayman. The roads of Britain were infested with gentlemen bent on earning a dishonest penny. They persecuted the unwary Derbyshire traveller mercilessly. One such character, who only succeeded in extracting a poor harvest from his victims, had the audacity to hand back a shilling (5p), so that the travellers could tip the coachman.

The highwayman's poor relation, the footpad, was also active. Mr. Ledworth who was robbed on Osmaston Road in 1776 by four footpads who dragged him off his horse and emptied his pockets suffered a fate all too common at this time.

Pickpockets frequented fairs, markets and race meetings. Anne Williamson was typical.

Ann was caught at Malton Fair in Yorkshire. *The Derby Mercury* reports:

> 'On her person were found four plain gold rings, and one with a stone, and two sparks in it, and a gold necklace'.

Burglary and housebreaking were common offences. Sometimes these felonies took the form of mass trespasses. Mr. John Drinkwater, who lived at Bugsworth, was burgled by a gang of seventeen men in 1813. The *Mercury* reports that the burglars:

> 'were part of that misguided and wicked set of men who call themselves Luddites, and have been twisted in'.

Solo careers in crime were more typical. Thomas Hulley was sentenced to death in August 1754 for the terrible crime of breaking into the shop of Samuel and Jonathan Hodgkinson of Baslow, and carrying away several pieces of dressed leather. Reprieved for this offence, he was later executed for returning from transportation before his appointed time. Quite apart from these conventional crimes, committed for the purpose of economic or financial gain, there existed a category of offences that owed more to the working out of authority conflicts. There were, for example, periodic outbreaks of arson and cattle maiming in the early nineteenth century. A notable Derbyshire case was that concerning John Brown, Thomas Jackson, George Booth and John King. Their case is dealt with in more detail later in this book.

Some crimes were regarded as being morally defensible. Fish and game, the poachers argued, were the products of nature. A fish recognised no geographical boundaries, and did not, therefore, belong to the person on whose land the river it inhabited lay. There is evidence, too, that many villagers did not view game as property in the same way as they viewed money, silver plate or clothing.

The judiciary took a different view. The Game Laws became very strict as a consequence but were steadfastly ignored, to such an extent that poaching constituted one seventh of all offences by 1827.

The forces of law and order were impotent in the face of this crime wave. At the apex of the forces of justice in a county lay the Lord Lieutenant, the King's representative in the county. His authority was largely symbolic, but he commanded the militia, and appointed Justices of the Peace.

It was on the Justices of the Peace that the real responsibility for crime prevention devolved. They were usually wealthy landowners, and their duties were unpaid.

The J.P.s oversaw the Petty Sessions courts. Before them were brought offenders such as vagrants, petty thieves and people who had evaded bastardy orders.

Four times a year they presided over the Quarter Sessions. Here criminals from all over the county were brought to be tried for serious offences, such as poaching and robbery.

Very serious cases, would be dealt with by the Assizes. The

J.P.s would send prisoners to the county gaol, pending the arrival of the circuit judge, who would try capital offences such as murder, rape and highway robbery.

The J.P.s were, however, overworked. Quite apart from their judicial duties they were also responsible for such onerous tasks as overseeing the poor law, supervising the upkeep of roads, and fixing prices and wages.

The extent to which effective justice was achieved was thus determined by the individual J.P.'s enthusiasm for his law enforcement responsibilities.

To assist them in upholding the King's Peace the Justices had the support of the parish constables. These constables were appointed by the J.P.s, or elected by the ratepayers. They had the power to arrest criminals, investigate crimes, and raise the hue and cry. But they were part-timers, employed as farmers or shopkeepers for most of the day, so they had little time for promenading around their village.

While it was possible to have a fairly clear idea of what was happening in a small rural village with a stable population, it became almost impossible in the rapidly growing urban centres, which were becoming flooded with 'foreigners'.

In these larger towns watchmen were employed, but they were often inefficient, and because of their low pay, were easily bribed. The Charlies, as they were derisively called, were also pretty thin on the ground, (they numbered only two thousand in London, which had a population at this time of about one million), so there were too few of them to have any effect on the crime rate.

In these circumstances, the public-spirited citizens of a town would often band together to form an Association for the Prosecution of Felons. These self-help organisations would offer rewards for the recovery of property or the apprehension of criminals.

The Mercury of 24 March 1803, contains an example of the type of notice common at this time:

> 'South Wingfield Association. Whereas some evil disposed person, or persons did on the night of the 12th, or on the morning of the 13th day of March instant, feloniously, take, steal and carry away

> *eleven pounds of yarn, part bleached from the orchard of Mr. John Lister of Pentridge Common, in the County of Derby, a member of the Association. This is to give notice that whosoever will give information to Mr. Wilson of Carnsfield, of the person, and persons, who committed the said robbery, shall on conviction receive a reward of five guineas from the said John Lister, above the reward allowed by the said Association.*
> *William Wilson, Agent and Treasurer, March 19, 1803'.*

The associations would also pay the costs of bringing a criminal to book. This was important, as the state did not normally prosecute felons, but would only act on behalf of private individuals bringing accusations.

These institutions proved hopelessly inadequate when confronted with the eighteenth century crimewave. In the absence of effective prevention, the authorities fell back on repression. They relied on deterring prospective criminals by threatening them with a criminal code which stipulated the death penalty for offences which would be regarded as trivial today.

Fifty offences had been punishable by death in 1689. By 1800 there were over two hundred capital offences. Capital punishment was now extended to such heinous crimes as inpersonating a Chelsea pensioner, chopping down trees, breaking down river banks and sending threatening letters, as well as being available for crimes such as murder, rape and high treason.

The 'Bloody Code', as it became known, had protection of property as its prime consideration. The laws of the land were framed by the propertied classes with their own interests very much in mind.

Thus pick-pockets, who stole money to the value of one shilling, faced the ultimate penalty, while people convicted of manslaughter were treated comparitively lightly. Fatalities occasioned by duelling, for example, were often treated as if they were different from the crime of murder, although the law made no such distinction.

The Cuddie affair, the most famous duelling incident in Derbyshire's criminal history, illustrates the leniency usually accorded to those indulging in this practice.

This crime aroused a great deal of excitement in the summer of 1821. Mr. William Cuddie, a surgeon residing in Winster had formed an attachment with one of his patients, Miss Brittlebank, the daughter of a solicitor living in the same village.

The young lady's family and friends disapproved of the relationship and tried to persuade Cuddie to relinquish any romantic ambitions he might harbour.

Cuddie met the lady, who was accompanied by her brother William, one day whilst out walking. William took offence at something Mr. Cuddie said, which he believed to be insulting to his sister. He sent the surgeon a letter demanding satisfaction for the insult. Cuddie ignored this proposal, but was persuaded that his honour as a gentleman was at stake.

A mutual friend, Edmund Spencer, tried to persuade William to apologise, but he refused. The duel took place at Oddo, Cuddie's house. Brittlebank and Cuddie used pistols. They stood 16 yards apart, and fired on a signal. Cuddie received a pistol ball in the stomach, and died the next day.

William Brittlebank fled the country, leaving his brothers, Andrew and Francis Brittlebank, and Edmund Spencer, to face the consequences. The three men had to stand trial for wilful murder, as they had aided and abetted William in the crime.

Although the facts of the

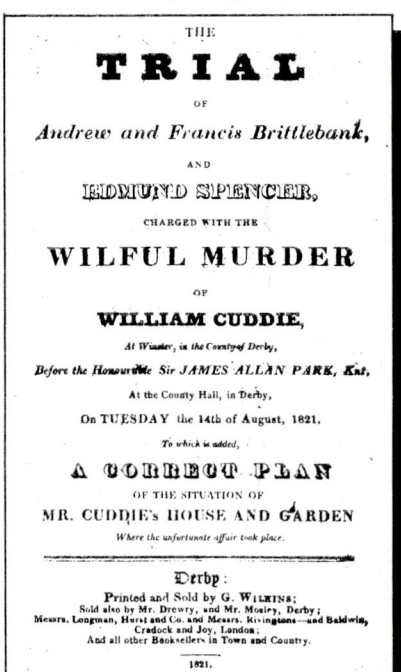

A pamphlet relating to the trial of the Brittlebanks and Edmund Spencer for the murder of William Cuddie
Derby Central Library
Local Studies Department

case were plain, the defendants successfully argued that the participants had only played a minor part in the proceedings, and were genuinely contrite about Cuddie's death. They were all acquitted after a sympathetic summing up by the judge.

Common criminals, however, received little sympathy. Sixty-eight people in Derbyshire were executed between 1732 and 1833, the overwhelming majority for economic crimes. Only twenty-six criminals were executed for non-economic crimes, and only thirteen of these had committed the crime of murder.

Although in theory many criminals were liable to the death penalty, in practice only a small proportion of those convicted actually had to pay the penalty prescribed by law. Eighteenth century judges had wide powers of discretion, and they would often decide to reprieve the culprits on their own initiative. In many cases this occurred before the Assizes judges actually left the town. Of four hundred and eighty people sentenced to death in 1832, for example, only thirty four actually suffered execution.

At the Assizes held in Derby on 19th March 1794, the judge sentenced to death the following people; Thomas Wilson, alias John Wood, for stealing a mare, John Pearce, alias Pares, for housebreaking, John and Thomas Watson, for stealing one sheep, James Barnes, for breaking open a box and stealing $19\frac{1}{2}$ guineas (£20.47), and Owen Murray, James Murray, and Michael Rock for housebreaking.

The judge, however, was 'pleased' to reprieve all but James Murray.

The judge made an example of one or two prisoners to show that the threat of death was real, but stopped well short of the mass executions that he could have initiated, had he so desired.

But the fact that the capital penalty was resorted to only very infrequently made it an ineffective deterrent. The criminal was encouraged to believe that even if he was convicted of a capital offence, a prison sentence or transportation, rather than death would be the more likely punishment.

To this could also be added the likelihood that the jury

SENTENCES OF THE PRISONERS,

Confined in his Majesty's Gaols for the COUNTY *of* DERBY, *who have taken their Trials at the Assizes, commencing on* Tuesday, August 7, 1827, *before the* RIGHT HONOURABLE CHARLES LORD TENTERDEN, *Chief Justice of our Lord the King, assigned to hold Pleas before the King himself, and the* HONOURABLE SIR GEORGE SOWLEY HOLROYD, *Knight, one of the Justices of our said Lord the King, assigned to hold Pleas before the King himself.*

EDWARD SACHEVERELL CHANDOS POLE, of RADBORNE, Esq. HIGH-SHERIFF.

NO.	PRISONERS NAME, AGE, WHEN AND BY WHOM COMMITTED.	CRIME.	SENTENCE.
1	THOMAS SHAW, aged 20. March 31, 1827. *S. Frith and G. W. Newton, Esqrs.*	Feloniously stealing in the parish of Gloosopp, a grey mare, the property of Henry Handford.	*Judgment of Death Recorded.*
2	WILLIAM BOWN, aged 21. April 30, 1827. *Philip Gell, Esq.*	Stealing from a close in Kirk Ireton, five sheep, the property of Joseph Matkin.	*Judgment of Death Recorded.*
3	WILLIAM CROSSLAND, aged 17. May 2, 1827. *Robert Arkwright, Esq.*	Wilfully, maliciously and unlawfully cutting Elisha Walton at the parish of Bakewell, with a sharp instrument, with an intent to do him some grievous bodily harm.	*Judgment of Death Recorded.*
4	WILLIAM CROSSLAND, aged 17. (*The last mentioned Prisoner.*)		
5	JAMES BURGIN, aged 21.	Stealing from the person of Edward Fletcher, at Bakewell, one leather pocket book and two country bank notes of the value of one pound each, the property of the said Edward Fletcher.	*No. 5 and 6—Transported for life.*
6	GEORGE LEE, aged 28. July 12, 1827. *M. M. Middleton and G. Crompton, Esqrs.*		
7	THOMAS BRADBY, aged 29. May 29, 1827. *William Webster, Esq.*	Feloniously breaking into a corn mill at Wirksworth Bank, in the parish of Wirksworth, and stealing therefrom eighteen strokes of wheat thrashed and winnowed, intermixed with oats, the property of Thomas Fowk.	*Imprisoned six months, and kept to hard labour.*
8	JOHN BURNS, aged 23. May 31, 1827. *J. Jebb and G. Crompton, Esqrs.*	Violently and feloniously assaulting Caroline Ann Hinde, at the parish of Chesterfield, and against her will then and there feloniously did ravish and carnally know.	*Acquitted.*
9	HANNAH EATHERINGTON, 32. June 1, 1827. *A. N. E. Mosley, Esq.*	Stealing out of the dwelling house of Robert Barton, of Hilton, two sovereigns, and eight shillings and sixpence in silver coin; and with stealing on various occasions within ten weeks then past, a quantity of ribbon, some Irish cloth, flannel, stockings, muslin, a shawl, a handkerchief, four neckerchiefs, a blue-linen apron, an Irish cloth apron, some lace cap crowns, a collar, and a new gown, of the value of forty shillings.	*Transported seven years.*
10	WILLIAM CLARKE, aged 23. July 18, 1827. *B. F. Forester, Esq. M. D.*	Stealing at Sandiacre, one pocket book, containing eight pounds, and a black canvas purse containing six shillings in silver, the property of John Coffin.	*Transported seven years.*
11	THOMAS DUNNICLIFF, aged 62. July 20, 1827. *Henry S. Wilmot, Esq.*	Stealing a piece of chesnut wood, at the parish of Melbourne, the property of the Right Honorable Penniston Lamb Viscount Melbourne.	*Imprisoned one month, and kept to hard labour.*
12	JOHN THOMPSON, aged 22. July 25, 1827. *G. Crompton, Esq.*	Breaking into the dwelling house of Thomas Heald, at Bolsover, at three o'clock in the morning, and stealing an invoice or bill of parcels.	*Imprisoned nine months, and kept to hard labour.*
13	JOHN JEPSON, aged 46. July 26, 1827. *G. B. Strutt, Esq.*	Stealing out of a stack yard at Belper, five sheaves of wheat straw thatch, the property of Samuel Harrison.	*Acquitted.*
14	PATRICK MAHON, aged 19. August 6, 1827. *J. J. Shuttleworth & James Holsworthy, Esqrs.*	Assaulting John Snape upon the highway in the parish of Hope, putting him in fear and danger of his life, and stealing from his person a one-pound country bank note, a sovereign, three silk handkerchiefs, and a shirt.	*Judgment of Death Recorded.*
15	JAMES NEAGLE, aged 29. August 6, 1827. *William Webster, Esq.*	Stealing out of the dwelling house of Welton Redshaw, in the parish of Bradford, a pair of silver spoons, and two tea spoons, the property of Reuben Redshaw.	*Acquitted.*
16	JAMES BOYNE, aged 42.	Stealing two sovereigns and a half at Ilam, the property of Charles Baines.	

Sentences of the prisoners at the August Assizes in 1827. Those prisoners who are recorded as receiving Judgement of Death would have a lesser sentence substituted.   *Derby Central Library Local Studies Department* themselves would be sympathetic. Many juries were reluctant to convict for crimes which would result in the death penalty. As a consequence, they would often find the defendants not guilty of capital offences, and they would go completely free. Alternatively, they could find the prisoner guilty of stealing a sum of money below that subject to the capital penalty, instead of for the actual amount stolen.

The prospect of enduring a public execution does not seem to have been a great deterrent to the eighteenth century criminal. Sometimes crime actually took place under the gallows itself.

At the execution of William Rose for horse-stealing, on 15 April 1784, the *Derby Mercury* could report:

> 'An amazing concourse of people assembled at the tree, it being Easter Fair, amongst them a farmer, almost under the gallows, who had his pockets picked of upwards of £8'.

In any case, the prospect of death was not likely to dissuade people made desperate by hunger and unemployment. They simply had nothing to lose.

The majority of the Derbyshire criminals arraigned at the Quarter Sessions were not professional criminals but people who stole petty articles, such as food, clothes, and even old shoes. Anything, in fact, that would fetch small sums of money, and prevent destitution.

John Rushton was capitally convicted of stealing from Mr. Thomas Smith of Mayfield a yellow and white shirt in March 1785, for example.

To land in court could be a harrowing experience for poor people accused of theft. They were often illiterate, found it difficult to defend themselves, and they were not automatically granted the services of an attorney.

Criminals of high social status were often treated leniently compared to their working class cousins, but certain categories of crimes, such as forgery, were regarded as especially reprehensible, and no mercy was extended to these found guilty.

The case of Charles Pleasants illustrates this, and also

shows the psychological torture to which Pleasants was subjected. The *Mercury* presents the story as follows:

> 'Great interest is making to obtain a reprieve, a petition signed by many of the gentlemen, and tradesmen of this place being sent to London for that purpose, as tis said to be the first act of this kind he had committed, and his behaviour in prison having rendered him an object of compassion'.

On 8 April Pleasants was respited. Mr. Hinde, one of the King's messengers, brought the message. Hinde had fallen from his horse, and arrived at eight on the Friday, just in time to save Pleasants who was to be hung at midday:

> 'All the apparatus of death being prepared, having his shroud on, and also a headstone coffin ready for him in the room'.

But the unfortunate man's agonies were not yet over, on the 24th he received a letter assuring him that the judge had made a favourable report, and that he might expect to be transported for life. On the 25th an order was received to execute him. The *Mercury* said:

> 'So extraordinary an instance of this kind is not remembered by the oldest person in Derby, for it may be compared to executing him twice, and which is much more shocking to him, the time preceding his death is shorter than is usual in such cases'.

This time there was to be no reprieve and Pleasants was executed on 4 May.

Some crimes evoked a sympathetic response from the public.

On 22 March 1834, 21 miners from the Magpie mine appeared at the Spring Assizes charged with the murder of three miners from the neighbouring Red-Soil mine.

The two mines adjoined, and the miners were in dispute over a vein of lead. The dispute had a long history, and had never been satisfactorily settled. Feelings were running high in August 1833, and the Red-Soil men took the fateful decision to smoke out the Magpie men, by lighting straw at the place where they descended. The smoke caused some discomfort, but not enough to cause the miners to desist from their operations.

The Magpie men were outraged, and they decided to retaliate. They purchased a quantity of Sulphur and oil of coal and on 2 September they succeeded in starting a more serious fire, with disastrous consequences. Three of the Red-Soil miners, Francis Taylor, Isaac Bagshaw and Thomas Wager, died, and several others only escaped suffocation by falling into the water.

Henry Knowles, the Red-Soil overseer, stopped up the top of the mine when he heard of the Magpie men's activities. This had the effect of cutting off the airflow, and prevented the smoke from rising, thus allowing it to escape through the engine shaft, saving the lives of those who were furthest away.

The Magpie men were summoned to learn the consequences of their stupidity at the Spring Assizes, where they were charged that they:

> *'feloniously, wilfully of their malice aforethought suffocated and murdered Francis Taylor, Isaac Bagshaw and Thomas Wager'.*

There was sympathy for the accused men from the start. Even the prosecution recognised that the charges were unnecessarily harsh. Sergeant Goulbourne, for the prosecution, said:

> *'It is a case which appears to run very closely upon that line which distinguishes manslaughter from murder, and those who instruct me to seek not the blood of the prisoners, but are merely anxious that justice be satisfied, incline to the milder conclusion'.*

As the story unfolded the judge, Mr. Justice Littledale, directed that several of the defendants be acquitted, as there appeared to be very little evidence that they had participated in the incidents.

Douglas Fox, a Derby surgeon, said that in his opinion the men had died as a result of concussion occasioned by falling rather than suffocation, and Mr. Justice Littledale informed the jury that if they were satisfied that the deceased died in this way the indictment against the accused had not been proven.

In his summing up he stressed that the jury must be sure that all the defendants were in the mine on the day of the fire, and they also had to be confident that the men were in that part of the mine where the fire had been started, and not in any other.

With this advice to ponder, the jury left to consider their verdict. It took them only ten minutes to find the Magpie men not guilty, a verdict which was generally hailed with relief by the citizens of Derby.

This case is exceptional, however. On the whole murder was generally regarded as the most terrible of all crimes, and murderers (and murderesses) received little sympathy from the public.

Murderers were hardly ever reprieved in the eighteenth and early nineteenth centuries, and it is a sobering fact that all of the criminals convicted of murder at Derbyshire Assizes in the period 1732-1833 were subsequently executed.

Murderers do not figure heavily in the Assize calendars, but it is difficult to gauge the incidence of murder, which was undoubtedly higher than the calendars suggest. Unless the murder victim had an established relationship with their killer it was difficult to detect the culprit.

Infanticide and concealment of birth were also common crimes in an era which required no issue of birth or death certificates.

To add to these difficulties forensic evidence was non-existent, and it was difficult to detect poison, for example, if the villains had only used the minimum needed to effect their purpose.

Sometimes the responsibility for a murder would only be discovered by the confession of the perpetrators. George Lacey Powell and John Drummond, who were executed for highway robbery on 14 August 1801, confessed to the murder of a Mr. Hill, as he was returning from Alfreton market, as they stood on the scaffold awaiting execution.

The Winnats Pass murders is a more celebrated example. The story has passed into Derbyshire mythology, but there are few hard facts relating to the case.

The tale that has been handed down concerns a young Scottish couple called Allan and Clara. In the year 1748, facing parental opposition to their proposed marriage, the two lovers decided to elope, and undertook the long and dangerous journey from their native Scotland to the Peak Forest in Derbyshire. At this time the chapel in the Peak Forest performed the function of an eighteenth century Gretna Green. The vicar, due to some ecclesiastical anomaly, did not come under the jurisdiction of a bishop, and consequently he could marry couples immediately, at any hour of the day or night.

Eventually the weary travellers arrived at an inn in Castleton, and decided to seek directions from the landlord. They did not observe the four shifty looking characters who were engaged in a drinking bout in one corner of the Inn. But the men noticed them, and Allan's bulging saddlebag in particular.

They hatched a scheme to rob the couple. As Allan and Clara picked their way between the rocks on the winding path that lead through Winnats Pass, the four men pounced. Allan and Clara were brutally murdered with a pick axe and their bodies buried in a barn. The men, all miners, divided their booty and melted away into the night.

Four days later the couples horses were discovered. By now there was a strong presumption that the lovers were dead.

Ten years later two skeletons were discovered in the barn, and the fate of the unfortunate lovers was confirmed.

A vigorous investigation had been mounted at the time of the tragedy, but the murderers had never been apprehended. Their identity might never have come to light if it had not been for a series of misfortunes that befell them. One man was crushed by falling boulders in the Winnats, another fell to his death near the spot where the murder was committed, and yet a third went insane.

Finally the fourth man, pricked by his conscience, revealed the full story of the foul deed to the Vicar of Castleton whilst on his death bed.

Clara's saddle exhibited at the Speedwell Cavern gift-shop, Castleton
photograph: Philip Taylor

Clara's saddle can still be seen in the shop beside the entrance to the Speedwell Cavern.

Trials for murder attracted the greatest interest amongst afficionados. The Court in St. Mary's Gate became so crowded on these occasions that entry to the courtroom was restricted to ticket holders only, so that the gentry and tradesmen were not deprived of a view of the interesting proceedings.

Inside the courtroom the accused could expect to receive little help in organising their defence. They were not allowed to offer evidence, or cross examine witnesses. Until 1837, the prisoners did not automatically have the right to a lawyer to represent them, or to address the jury on their behalf.

Murder trials were often short, and if the defendants were found guilty thay had little time to appeal against the sentence, which could be carried out within two days.

Because of the rather indecent haste with which these proceedings were conducted many innocent people were to suffer execution.

Once all hope of a reprieve had gone, prisoners were exhorted by the prison chaplain to think of their spiritual salvation, to prepare themselves for the fate that awaited them, and to confess their sins so that they could be forgiven.

These confessions, together with details of the crime, were

sold as broadsheets at the scene of the execution, where they met with an enthusiastic response.

Samuel Drewry, who owned the *Derby Mercury*, produced many of these broadsheets. His first printings were for the execution of William Hewitt and Rosamund Ollerenshaw in 1732. His decendants at the *Mercury* were to carry on his good work, for broadsheets were to retain their popularity until the middle of the nineteenth century. The executions themselves, which were publicly held, were often brutal, due to the modus operandi of the hangman.

In eighteenth century Derby the condemned were conveyed to the execution on a cart. The rope was draped over the gallows tree, and around the culprits neck. At a given signal, the cart would move away leaving the unfortunate person suspended.

The application of this rather hit and miss method of execution resulted in many deaths occurring as a result of strangulation rather than from the dislocation of the neck.

The unfortunate Charles Pleasants, already encountered, was one victim of the hamgman's ineptitude. As the *Mercury* rather unfeelingly relates:

Derby County Hall, St. Mary's Gate, scene of many famous murder trials
photograph: Philip Taylor

'It was remarked by most people present that he struggled more than usual in such cases, owing, as it is said, to the slipping of the rope, which he himself had fixed, and which got under his chin, and is supposed to have occasioned him great pain'.

The construction of a drop at the new County Gaol in 1827 obviated the need for the horse and cart method, and thereafter executions became less messy.

After the body had been cut down it was, in accordance with the law, delivered to the surgeons for anatomical dissection. This requirement was particularly resented by the people who regarded the practice as being needlessly callous. The strength of this feeling can be gauged by Hogarth's illustrations, which represent dissection as one of the four stages of cruelty. This practice was continued until 1834.

Many victims were later buried in St. Peter's Churchyard, but those murderers who were convicted of particularly shocking crimes could be displayed on a gibbet.

This, then, was the likely pattern of events for those unfortunate enough to come before the Assize Judges, at the County Hall in St. Mary's Gate.

We now turn to the stories of the men and women who were to suffer the ultimate penalty for their crimes.

A List of People Executed During the Period 1732 - 1837

Name	Crime	Date of Execution
John Hewitt and Rosamund Ollerenshaw	Murder	29 March 1732
John Smith	Burglary	August 1735
Richard Woodward	Highway Robbery	30 March 1738
William Dolphin	Highway Robbery	9 April 1740
George Ashmore	Coining	29 August 1740
Robert Bowler	Attempted Murder	1 August 1741
Mary Dilks	Murder	23 March 1754
Anne Williamson	Picking Pockets	1 August 1755
John Ratcliffe	Horsestealing	12 April 1756

Thomas Halley	Returning from Transportation	29 April 1757
Charles Kirkman	Murder	24 March 1759
John Perry and Amos Mason	Highway Robbery	12 August 1763
John Lowe	Housebreaking	20 April 1768
Matthew Cocklayne	Murder	21 March 1776
James Meadows	Highway Robbery	31 March 1780
William Buxton	Highway Robbery	25 August 1780
James Williams	Horsestealing	28 March 1782
John Shaw	Breaking out of Gaol	2 August 1782
Thomas Greensmith	Burglary	8 April 1784
William Rose	Horsestealing	16 April 1784
William Grooby, George Grooby and James Peet	Housebreaking	15 March 1785
John Shepherd	Housebreaking	7 April 1786
William Stanley	Burglary	7 April 1786
James Halliburton	Rape	2 September 1786
John Porson	Picking Pockets	16 April 1787
Thomas Grundy	Murder	29 March 1788
Joseph Allen	Burglary	20 August 1790
William Rider	Rape and Robbery	8 April 1791
James Murray	Housebreaking	4 April 1794
Thomas Neville	Highway Robbery	10 April 1795
James Preston	Murder	25th March 1796
James Gratton	Burglary	14 August 1796
John Dent	Sheep Stealing	14 August 1796
John Evens	Robbery	14 August 1796
Thomas Knowles	Uttering a Note	5 September 1800
George Lacy Powell and John Drummond	Highway Robbery	14 August 1801
James Mellor and Thomas Spencer	Burglary	27 August 1802
William Wells	Murder	19 March 1803
Richard Booth, John Parker and John Tolly	Horsestealing	6 April 1804

William Webster	Murder	26 March 1807
Joseph West	Forgery	8 April 1807
Percival Cook and James Tomlinson	Burglary	10 April 1812
Paul Mason, Richard Hibbert and Paul Henshaw	Burglary	9 April 1813
Anthony Lingard	Murder	28 March 1815
Joseph Wheeldon	Murder	9 August 1816
John Brown, George Booth, Thomas Jackson and John King	Arson	14 August 1817
Jeremiah Brandreth, Isaac Ludlam and John Turner	High Treason	7 November 1817
Hannah Bocking	Murder	22 March 1819
Thomas Hopkinson	Highway Robbery	2 April 1819
Hannah Halley	Murder	22 April 1822
George Batty	Rape	8 April 1825
George Leedham	Bestiality	12 April 1833

Chapter II

THE BLOODY CODE

The case of Hewitt and Ollerenshaw is the first murder story recorded by the *Derby Mercury*.

In 1732, the landlady of the Crown public house at Nuns Green had embarked on a love affair with John Hewitt, a butcher. Hewitt, a married man, not content with this affair had added to his already complicated love life by sampling the favours of Rosamund Ollerenshaw, the landlady's servant.

The three of them hatched a plot to dispose of Hewitt's wife, Hannah, so that these relationships could continue unhindered.

Rosamund's employer prepared a pancake liberally sprinkled with poison, which Rosamund took to Mrs. Hewitt. Hannah obligingly consumed this, and died in agony three hours later.

Rosamund and John were the obvious suspects, and were immediately taken into custody.

They were found guilty at their trial, but the landlady escaped her just desserts due to lack of evidence.

Prior to her execution, Rosamund confessed to the killing of her illegitimate child. The authorities investigated her story, and on examining the area indicated by her the bones of a child of about seven months were discovered.

Drewy, the printer of the *Derby Mercury*, brought out a confession on the morning of the execution. The paper reported that:

> 'A vast number of people pitied, and prayed for them. They were both executed in their shrouds, which added to the awfulness of the sight'.

A spectator to their last hours was the Derby historian,

William Hutton, then a nine year old boy. Hutton records that the crowd was so immense and unruly that he was nearly knocked into the brook at Nuns Green.

John Smith, was tried at Derbyshire Assizes in July 1735, for breaking into the house of Mr. Bowyer, of Roston, and stealing a silver cup.

Smith, a native of Norbury, was found guilty and subsequently executed.

The *Mercury's* account of his execution consists mainly of a diatribe against Roman Catholicism, and gives us an insight into the religious intolerance of that age.

The *Mercury* declares that John Smith was:

> 'an illiterate man, and understood little of religion'.

After his condemnation he was visited by a man who:

> 'passes under the character of a Popish priest'.

> 'So industrious it seems is the Popish faction to make proselytes, especially of late in these parts, as well as others, that even an illiterate housebreaker, whose life was no credit to any communion, must at last, by all means, be prevailed upon to die a Catholic, and what he meant by that word, is easy to be understood'.

Highway robbery was a common crime in the eighteenth century, and there were many local exponents. One such was Richard Woodward. He was aided by an accomplice called James Giddens, who arrived at the gallows in Nottingham in 1737, ahead of his companion in infamy.

Richard was condemned at the March Assizes 1738, and was executed two days later.

Another Derbyshire gentleman of the roads was William Dolphin whose crime was that, together with James Hill, he robbed Mr. Lord on the highway, near Chesterfield, of a considerable sum of money. Both Dolphin and Hill were condemned for this offence at the Assizes on 27 March 1740, but Hill was later reprieved, mainly it appears because he had stated that Dolphin was the chief instigator of the scheme.

The thirty-three year old Dolphin kept his appointment with the hangman on 9 April, denying his guilt to the last.

George Ashmore was a counterfeiter. He was executed on 29 August 1740, and buried in Sutton-on-the-Hill churchyard. From here, perhaps due to the machinations of some eighteenth century resurrection man, the body was shortly afterwards stolen.

Robert Bowler was tried before Lord Chief Baron Probyn, on 28th July 1741, for shooting and dangerously wounding Edward Rivington, a butcher, as he was returning from Belper to Pentrich.

Found guilty, he was executed on 1 August, after declaring his innocence to the crowd.

On a cold morning in January 1754 the body of a newborn child was found on a sandbank, near the Holmes, at Derby.

Suspicion soon developed on Mary Dilks, and she was taken before the magistrates on 8th January for examination.

Mary initially laid the blame on another woman. This woman, she said, had delivered her child, and then disappeared taking the baby with her. The magistrates were unconvinced, and having checked her story questioned her again on 14th January.

The Howard Hotel, Friar Gate. The old County Prison, erected in 1756, stood on this site. *photograph: Philip Taylor*

This time, Mary said that the baby had been born on 1st January, and had died soon after birth. She admitted that her previous statement implicating the other woman was incorrect, and the magistrates ordered her to be detained in the County Gaol, until the next Assizes.

This took place on 21st March, before Mr. Justice Birch, and after a three hour trial Mary was found guilty, and sentenced to death.

She confessed her guilt to the chaplain shortly before her execution, which took place two days after the trial. The execution attracted large crowds, as Mary was the first woman to be executed in Derby for more than twenty years.

After execution, her body was given over to the surgeons for dissection.

Another woman unfortunate enough to suffer the full rigour of the law was Anne Williamson, alias Sparrow alias Knowls, the Malton Fair pickpocket, who had been apprehended with a fine assortment of jewellery about her person. Ann had

St. Peter's Churchyard, Derby. Many executed criminals were buried here in the eighteenth century. *photograph: Philip Taylor*

previously escaped from Derby Gaol on 21st February 1755, where she was awaiting trial for picking George White's pocket at Ashbourne Fair. A reward of ten pounds for her capture had led to her discovery at Malton, and she was returned to Derby to await trial. Justice Penman sentenced her to death on 24th July for 'pocketing' six guineas (£6.30) and one thirty-six shillings (£1.80), the property of George White.

At her execution on 1st August 1755 she acknowledged the justice of the sentence, and asked all young people to take warning from her fate. Anne was buried in St. Peters Churchyard.

Horsestealing was another profitable, though dangerous occupation as John Retcliff was to discover. Retcliff stole two grey horses, from a close near Lichfield, and was brought before Sir Sydney Stafford-Smythe, who sentenced him to death. The execution was carried out on 12th April 1756.

Thomas Hulley had been transported for seven years for the offence of housebreaking. He returned before this period had expired and was sentenced to death, along with John Retcliff's brother Thomas, at the March Assizes 1757.

A great deal of sympathy was extended to him, and a petition was got up, the citizens of Derby feeling that the penalty was excessive.

A reprieve was not forthcoming, however, and Hulley walked to his fate on 29th April.

On 27th February, 1759, the body of Sarah Hall's newborn infant child was found in the Gaolbrook. Sarah was taken before the magistrates but was released, after being vigorously cross-examined.

Her lover, Charles Kirkman, now became the chief suspect, and he was promptly arrested.

Kirkman was tried before Baron Smythe on 19th March, and was executed on 24th March, maintaining his innocence even on the scaffold.

John Perry and Amos Mason were sentenced to death by

Lord Mansfield, the Lord Chief Justice, on 28th July, 1763, for robbing Mr. Staveley on the highway. They were executed on 12th August.

John Lowe was sentenced to the final penalty of the law for housebreaking. Several Methodists attended John at his execution on 20th April 1768.

Charles Pleasants' case has already been dealt with earlier in this book. He was executed on 4th May 1768.
"amidst an almost incredible number of spectators".

Matthew Cocklayne was the son of a tanner, and was born in Ireland. At the tender age of thirteen he joined the army, serving for ten years, with credit, before being discharged.

Matthew settled in Derby, and married, but having made the acquaintance of George Foster he embarked on a career of petty crime.

In 1774, he became friendly with a servant girl, who worked for a Mrs. Vickers in Full Street. This girl told him that the lady kept a great amount of money in the house.

Their appetites thus whetted, the two miscreants decided to burgle the house. Cocklayne, apparently, got in through a window at the back of the house and facilitated Foster's entry. Then they went upstairs, where Cocklayne clubbed Mrs. Vickers with an iron pin, killing her. The pair decamped with £300 and the rings from Mrs. Vickers' house.

However, they were seen by one of the servants, and Cocklayne threatened her.

The two men split up, arranging to meet later. Matthew went to Leek, before joining Foster again in Liverpool.

The two took ship to Ireland, and tried their hand at highway robbery. At this they were singularly unsuccesful. Foster was shot, and died of his injuries, while Cocklayne was captured, and brought back to Derby to stand trial.

The evidence against him was circumstantial, and Cocklayne was fairly confident that he would get off. But the maid's testimony, weighed heavily against him, and he was convicted of murder at the March Assizes, 1776.

He was hanged before a large crowd on 21st March. Instead of being dissected his body was hung in chains at Bradshaw street, as an object to others tempted to commit similar crimes.

James Meadows, aided by an accomplice, robbed William Featherstone of Alstonefield on the highway at Newhaven, near Ashbourne, of thirty-seven golden guineas (£38.85) and three shillings (15p) in silver.

Sir James Eyre put an end to his career after he was convicted of the crime at the March Assizes in 1780.

A curiosity of the execution was that Meadows was forced to pray in the coach of the executioner, because a hailstorm prevented the customary prayers on the scaffold.

William Buxton committed the mistake of robbing the Manchester Stage of seven pounds at Newhaven. Unfortunately for him he was followed, and arrested in Ashbourne. Buxton had a long criminal history, having previously robbed a post-chaise and deserted from Colonel Fullerton's regiment. After previous offences in 1778 Buxton had been sent to the Thames hulks, from where he subsequently escaped. He had even been arrested on his wedding day, for forging a draft on his master, but had been acquitted.

Justice Ashurst brought his unsavoury career to an end at the August Assizes 1780, but even while he lay under sentence of death Buxton was plotting his escape. A friend brought tools to him in prison, but later repented and told the gaoler.

Buxton's luck finally ran out for him on 25th August at the gallows tree, for there was to be no miraculous escape from this situation.

Francis Butler passed sentence of death on James Williams, alias John Green at the March Assizes, 1782, for stealing a dark brown gelding of the value of fifteen guineas (£15.75) from Mr. Worthington of Altrincham. Williams was executed on 28th March 1782, dying without a struggle.

It is reported that he nonchalantly sucked an orange while awaiting the final preparations for his end.

John Shaw received the capital sentence at the same Assizes as James Williams, but had been reprieved. Shaw's crime had been to burgle Mr. Anthony Goodwin of Wirksworth, taking a watch from the house.

On 22nd April, Shaw, together with three other felons, Edward Johnson, William Lee and William Cupitt, broke out of gaol. He then embarked on a brief, but frenetic, series of burglaries, robbing two houses on the 23rd April, and four houses at Wirksworth on the 25th. Finally Shaw stole a horse at Hopton, but was apprehended at Spend Lane, near Ashbourne.

On the 19th of July, Shaw and his fellow escapees received sentence of death from Lord Chief Justice Loughborough for breaking out of gaol.

Cupitt and Johnson were quickly reprieved, leaving only Shaw and Lee for execution. Eventually Lee was respited after a petition by the High Sheriff and the Grand Jury, leaving the unfortunate Shaw, who was twenty-one, to a lonely execution on 2nd August 1782.

Thomas Greensmith and William Rose were convicted at the Spring Assizes 1784 before Sir Thomas Eyre. Greensmith's crime had been to rob Rea and Company of Walton-on-Trent of plate. He was executed on 8th April under the following unfortunate circumstances.

> "When the cart drew away, he slid down very gently, and lifted his hand to the rope for a very short time, when his hold failing he was after a few struggles launched into eternity".

William Rose was executed on 16th April for horse-stealing, befor a large crowd.

Two brothers, John and Benjamin Jones, were condemned for burglary at the Summer Assizes 1784. They cheated the hangman by performing the service themselves, using cords from their irons wound around the roof beams.

William Grooby, George Grooby and James Peet, broke into the shop of Samuel Leam of Pentrich, for which crime they had to pay with their lives. Justice Heath ordered their execution at the Spring Assizes on 15th March 1785.

The men were apparently very sensible of their situation, and very contrite. Whilst awaiting execution James Peet wrote on the cell door in chalk,

> "Calm and composed my soul a journey takes,
> no guilt that troubles, nor a heart that aches".

John Shepherd and William Stanley were sentenced to death, in accordance with the law, at the Assizes in March 1786 by Mr. Justice Heath. Shepherd had broken into the house of Mr. Smith of Sandiacre, and Stanley had committed a burglary.

On 7th April they were executed. Stanley had previously made himself a noose out of a large handkerchief, presumably because he wished to emulate the Jones brothers. He was later interred in St. Peter's Churchyard. Shepherd showed more composure, nodding and waving to old acquaintences at the scene of the execution.

James Halliburton, a corporal in the Fifth Regiment of foot, was indicted at the summer Assizes 1786 for raping Millicent Smith, the wife of a Biggin farmer.

Halliburton had a six hour trial before Sir Henry Gould, on 8th August. His officers gave him a good character reference, but the Judge said the case was aggravated by the brutality shown by Halliburton.

He was executed on 2nd September 1786.

John Porson, a youth of nineteen, was apprehended after picking John Johnson's purse of eight guineas (£8.40) and eleven shillings (55p) in Town Street, Ashbourne.

Porson had put the purse back, but had been observed doing it, and he had to pay the supreme penalty of the law on 16th April 1787.

Thomas Grundy, a tailor by occupation, lived with his

brother's family at Dale Abbey. In November, 1787, for motives which remain obscure, he poisoned his brother and fled to Nottingham. Here, in an effort to disguise himself, he sold his clothes and bought some new ones.

He was arrested and brought back to Derby for trial.

This took place on 17th March 1788, before Baron Thomson, and after five and a half hours Grundy was found guilty. On 29th March he was executed, after trying to implicate his niece. The *Mercury* reports that the twenty year old Grundy was,

> "obliged to lean upon the executioner, crying very bitterley".

Joseph Allen's crime was to steal two silver candlesticks from the house of Tom Barker in the Cornmarket, Derby. Allen protested his innocence and,

> "he was turned off denying the fact for which he suffered on 20th August 1790".

William Rider is described as well educated. He suffered on 8th April 1791, for the dual crime of ravishing Mary Barton, near Makeney toll bar, and robbing her of 3d (1¼p). He was tried only for the second crime and received the capital penalty! The twenty-two year old Rider did not relish the fate in store for him, and on the Sunday before the execution he removed his irons, and had succeeded in climbing the wall before he was detected.

On the following Friday, William was executed. The scene itself was an affecting one, as Rider was weak from long imprisonment and could hardly stand. The *Mercury* reports that,

> "many of the spectators, and those unaccustomed to weep, were in tears, saying that it was one of the most poignant spectacles they had ever seen".

James Murray, Owen Murray and Michael Rock were convicted of housebreaking at the March Assizes 1794. Only James, who was a Roman Catholic, suffered the ultimate penalty, which took place on 4th April.

Thomas Neville was also a Catholic. He does not appear to have taken his spiritual salvation too seriously, however, for he assaulted John Morley on the Derby highway on 2nd January 1795 removing from his person fourteen and a half golden guineas (£15.22½), and some silver.

His appointment with the hangman was on 10th April, but it seems to have had little deterrent effect on the spectators, for the *Mercury* reports that,

> "Severall persons witnessing this awful scene had their pockets picked".

James Preston, aged 70, was executed for the murder of Susannah Moreton's illegitimate baby at Mickleover in February 1796.

Preston and Moreton were committed to the Spring Assizes over which Sir Giles Rooke presided on 15th March. They were both sentenced to death, but Susannah was reprieved on the morning of the execution, which took place on 25th March.

Thomas Knowles was found guilty at the Summer Assizes of feloniously uttering a note at Chesterfield, to the value of one guinea (£1.05) with intent to defraud Messrs. John and William Stone.

Great efforts were made to obtain a reprieve for Knowles, because the punishment was seen as excessive, and he succeeded in obtaining a respite for eighteen days. But the authorities felt that the crime was an extreme one, and the unfortunate Knowles was hanged on 5th September 1800.

Derby afficionados of the gallows' scenes were granted a rare treat on 14th August 1801, when five culprits met simultaneous ends.

They had been condemned at the July Assizes by Sir Giles Rooke and Mr. Justice Heath. George Lacy Powell and John Drummond had committed several highway robberies, and confessed to a murder for which they had not been tried on the gallows. James Gratton had burgled the house of Philip Yeomans of Shottle in March, stealing eight guineas (£8.40) and seven shillings, (35p), amongst other items. John Dent's offence was to steal two rams from Mr. Creswell of Ravenstone, while John Evans had dishonestly come into the possession of two sacks of oats belonging to Mr. Robottom of Duffield.

In the early nineteenth century, the Spencers, and their cousins the Mellors, appear to have regarded the pursuit of crime as a fitting family occupation. In 1802 James Mellor, 22, was convicted of stealing a pony from Mrs. Taylor of Wirksworth, and Tom Spencer junior, his thirty-one year old cousin was condemned for a burglary of the dwelling house of Mr. Flint of Biggin. George Spencer, another relative, had turned King's Evidence against them.

They were hanged on 27th August, showing little remorse for their crimes and, says the *Mercury*,

> "in their last moments exhibited an affecting proof of human depravity".

Tom Spencer senior, the father of Tom, was condemned at the Nottinghamshire Assizes at this time, but was reprieved.

William Wells was committed to the County Gaol for the murder of George Bingham at Barlborough, near Chesterfield.

He took his trial before Sir Robert Graham on 17th March 1803, and was convicted of the crime.

His execution, which took place on 19th March, must have been horrific, for, as the *Mercury* reports,

> "About a minute after he had been turned off, the rope slipped, and he fell to the ground so the executioner was under the necessity of tying him up a second time".

Richard Booth, John Parker and John Tolly, were companions in infamy. They were found guilty of stealing two black horses from Mr. Bayliss of Rathwood, and received sentence of death from Sir Giles Rooke.

Their response to the situation was mixed. John Parker was

believed to be extremely penitent, but Richard Booth, a forty year old 6'4" giant, who had been previously condemned on three different occasions, showed little remorse. They were executed on 6th April 1804.

William Webster was indicted for the murders of Mrs. Dakin and Mrs. Roe by administering poison. He also poisoned Tom Dakin, Jane Fearn and four other people at Parwich, near Ashbourne.

At the Derbyshire Assizes, held in March 1807, Webster was convicted. He admitted his guilt on the scaffold on 26th March.

The *Derby Mercury* provides little background information to the murders, but they do not seem to have had an economic motive. It seems likely that Webster was insane.

Joseph West was condemned at the same Assizes as Webster. He committed the crime of circulating forged bank notes, several of which were found on his person when he was apprehended. He appeared very penitent at the gallows on 8th April 1807.

Percival Cook and James Tomlinson were convicted of burglary and sentenced to death. They had been part of a gang that had burgled the house of Mr. Samuel Hunt at Ockbrook on 23rd December 1811, taking from it thirty-five pounds in notes.

The previous night they had entered the house of John Brentnall at Locko Grange, but had been driven off by Mr. Brentnall, his son, and a servant maid.

The pair were convicted after one of the band, Thomas Draper, turned King's Evidence. The other members of the band, James Jerram (alias Ockbrook Will), John Howitt, Andrew Scott and John England, who scouted out potential victims for the gang, were convicted, but received lesser sentences.

Cook received Draper in his cell, and forgave him, which was remarkably magnanimous in the circumstances. Cook and Tomlinson were executed on a new drop in front of Derby Gaol, on 10th April 1812.

Paul Mason, Richard Hibbert and Paul Henshaw, together with Joseph Hibbert and William Daniels, were convicted of burgling Mr. Drinkwater's house at Bugsworth in 1813.

The men were members of a group some seventeen strong, who were, the *Derby Mercury* believes, influenced by Luddism.

Mr. Drinkwater identified the five men, and two others who were subsequently acquitted. The three men claimed that there had been a case of mistaken identity, and persisted in claiming their innocence on the drop.

Hannah Oliver, a widow aged forty-eight, kept the turnpike gate at Wardlow Mires, near Tideswell. On 5th January 1815, she was strangled by Anthony Lingard, who stole several pounds, and a new pair of shoes, which with some money, he gave to a girlfriend whom he had made pregnant. Lingard tried to persuade the girl to accept the gifts, in exchange for fathering the child on another man, but she was suspicious and returned them.

She then turned King's Evidence against him. On 25th March, Lingard was found guilty and sentenced to death.

After his execution on 28th March his body was hung in

Wardlow Mires. Lingard's body was exhibited here on a gibbet in 1815.
photograph: Philip Taylor

chains at Wardlow, as a warning to others contemplating similar activities. The field where Lingards body was exhibited is still known as Gibbet Field.

Joseph Wheeldon was brought to the County Gaol on 11th May 1816, and indicted for the murder of Isaac Wheeldon, aged nine, and Mary Anne Wheeldon, at Hulland Ward.

Joseph had attacked them with a gorse-hook, with such ferocity that he had nearly severed their heads. He was observed in the execution of these shocking activities by the children's six year old brother, who told his mother.

The motive for these murders is not apparent. The nature of the murders, though, suggests some kind of mental breakdown. Wheeldon was executed on 9th August 1816.

John Brown, George Booth, Thomas Jackson and John King were convicted at the Summer Assizes, 1817, of firing hay and corn stacks, the property of Winfield Halton Esq., of South Wingfield.

Their crime appears to have been motivated by considerations of revenge. The areas around Pentrich and South Wingfield were subject to mass unemployment, due to the decline of framework knitting, and the region was rife with discontent.

The four were convicted after Thomas Hopkinson, a nineteen year old youth, turned King's Evidence against them.

The execution, which was otherwise untoward, was notable for the fact that while the customary hymn service was being conducted a heavy shower of rain forced two of the men to take shelter from the rain under an umbrella.

Jeremiah Brandreth, Isaac Ludlam and John Turner were leaders of the Pentrich revolt. The story of these misguided men has been told in great detail by John Stevens, in his excellent book 'England's Last Revolution', but briefly the facts are these.

The area around Pentrich harboured many bitter, men in 1817. Hunger and unemployment had made men desperate, and ready to consider radical solutions to their problems. Brandreth and his supporters had imbibed the philosophy of the Hampden clubs. They believed that only a democratic government led by working class men responsive to the wishes of the people would suffice. They also realised that this government would have to be imposed by force.

The moving light in the local revolutionary movement was Thomas Bacon, an old follower of Tom Paine. Bacon was a primitive socialist. He believed that property should be equalised, that the landed estates should be broken up, and that eight acres of land should be given to each man. Together with Jeremiah Brandreth, sometimes referred to as the Nottingham Captain, he was in touch with delegates from other areas who were contemplating a national rising on 9th June 1817.

Unfortunately for Brandreth and his Derbyshire followers, one of the delegates was a government spy called Oliver. Oliver's part in this affair was to be crucial, as he acted both as an informer and as an agent provocateur.

The whole plan was known to the government, and the local authorities were well aware of the plot. The town clerk of Nottingham was able to write,

> "My confidential clerk is on the lookout, near Pentridge, watching the result of old Bacon's threatened movements".

On 9th June, the Pentrich group set off, led by Brandreth and George Weightman, fondly believing that they were part of a wider movement, shortly to be joined by hundreds of men at Nottingham. En route, they stopped at farms and houses to requisition arms, and recruit volunteers to the cause. These 'volunteers' were often less than enthusiastic, and drifted away at the earliest opportunity.

At one such house, that of Mrs. Hepworth, they were refused admittance, and Brandreth shot dead Robert Walters, one of the servants.

To keep up the spirits of his dwindling band, Brandreth had to constantly exhort them to bear up. He promised them roast beef and ale when they got to Nottingham, and even a pleasure trip on the Trent. Even this enticing prospect failed to quell the grumbles of discontent, and the desertion rate accelerated.

In the morning, the band was spotted by a troop of cavalry, who charged them. The band scattered, and the leaders went into hiding.

Brandreth was captured at Bristol, trying to take ship to the United States, Ludlam was taken at Uttoxeter on 22nd July, while Thomas Bacon was apprehended at St. Ives on 15th August.

A special Assize was convened at Derby on 15th October, before the Lord Chief Baron, Sir Richard Richards. The result was a foregone conclusion.

The prosecution, organised by a Derby solicitor, William Lockett, included the Attorney General and the Solicitor General. The defence was entrusted to the redoubtable George Denman, later to become Lord Chief Justice, and John Cross.

Denman tried to persuade the jury that the offence was really one of riot, but it was to no avail. Brandreth, Ludlam, Turner and Weightman were sentenced to be hung, drawn, and quartered, though the quartering was to be waived on this occasion. Weightman was subsequently reprieved and sentenced to transportation, along with Thomas Bacon and the other chief conspirators.

The hangings of Brandreth and Turner on 7th November were uneventful, but we are informed that Ludlam died in much pain, for he was repeatedly convulsed after he had been 'thrown off'.

After the bodies had hung for an hour, they were cut down and beheaded.

When the executioner held up Brandreth's head, crying "Behold the head of a traitor, Jeremiah Brandreth", the crowd recoiled in horror. The grim ceremonies complete, the bodies were buried in one grave in St. Werburgh's Churchyard.

The block on which Brandreth, Turner and Ludlam were decapitated can be seen in Derby Museum.

A sixteen year old girl was committed to the County Gaol on 19th September 1818, charged with poisoning a fellow servant, Jane Grant of Litton.

Hannah Bocking's trial took place on 18th March 1819, before Sir James Burrough. She was convicted and sentenced to death.

Hannah had poisoned Jane out of revenge, after Jane had been given a position she herself had desired, but which she had failed to secure due to 'her unamiable temper and disposition'.

There was no hope of a reprieve, because the crime was obviously premeditated, Hannah having purchased the poison ten weeks before she had introduced it into the cake.

Hannah tried to implicate several of her relatives in the murder, but when all hope of a reprieve had gone, she retracted her accusations, and admitted that she alone had been responsible for the death of Jane.

She seemed indifferent to her fate, although this may have been because she was in a state of shock.

> "At the moment, when she was launched into eternity, an involuntary shuddering pervaded the assembled crowd, and although she excited little sympathy, a general feeling of horror was expressed that one so young should have been so guilty, and so insensible".

Thomas Hopkinson had turned King's Evidence against four arsonists in 1817 but his narrow escape on that occasion seems to have had little effect on his subsequent behaviour.

Accompanied by John Fletcher, he stopped William Bucknall on the turnpike road near Dronfield, and stole from him a purse containing twelve shillings and sixpence (62½p).

Hopkinson had been born at Ashover, but had moved to Woolley Moor as a youth. Here he made the acquaintance of Tom Jackson, who was two years older. Hopkinson was apprenticed to a weaver, but to this official occupation he added the more lucrative one of criminal.

With Jackson as his mentor, he swiftly progressed from poaching, through petty pilfering, to sheep stealing. He spent his ill-gotten gains on drink and 'loose women' in Sheffield.

Hopkinson was apprehended after the highway robbery, and sentenced to death at the Spring Assizes. This hardened criminal showed no remorse, and was executed on 2nd April 1819.

An interesting footnote to this case is that Jackson's father, disgusted at Hopkinson for turning King's Evidence against his son, volunteered to be the hangman.

Hopkinson may well have wished that he had taken up this offer, for the execution was not one of which the hangman could be proud. Hopkinson:

> *"was much convulsed, after the drop fell and he seemed to suffer much more than is usual on such occasions".*

Hannah Halley was indicted for the murder of her infant child in Brook Street, Derby and committed to the Assizes on 21st March 1822. Here she was convicted, and sentence of death was passed by Mr. Justice Best.

Hannah, who was thirty-one years old at the time of her conviction, had been born in Mansfield, but had moved to Derby. She was pregnant, and had been married seven weeks before to a man who was not the father of her child. At the time the murder occurred she was working at the mill at Darley Abbey.

Her landlady at Brook Street and a woman visitor heard a child's cry, and ran upstairs. They told Hannah they suspected her of giving birth to a child.

One of the women threatened to fetch a constable, and the other looked under the bed and found a large jug, over which a cloth had been thrown. Under the cloth lay the body of a badly scalded baby, which died four days later. Hannah said that the devil had caused her to do it, but the jury suspected that she was relieving herself of an unwanted child in a particularly brutal way.

The strain of the trial, and its outcome, made Hannah ill,

and the poor woman had to be virtually carried to the scaffold on 25th March 1822.

Hannah would undoubtedly have been acquitted of murder later in the century, and the crime of consealment of birth would have been substituted. This was punishable by a prison sentence of a few years.

George Leedham, a twenty year old feeble minded labourer from Yeldersley, near Ashbourne, was sentenced to death, for the crime of bestiality, by Sir John Bosanquet, on 3rd April 1833.

This punishment seems excessive to modern eyes, but in the nineteenth century there was little knowledge of psycho-sexual motivations. The offence was regarded as particularly heinous because it was 'unnatural', that is it offended against God, as well as the man, and therefore had to be punished very severely.

However, even the conservative *Mercury,* shocked though it was by the offence, conceded that the punishment was too severe.

Leedham was executed on 12th April, on the drop outside the New County Gaol, on Vernon Street, the first execution to take place at this spot.

George Batty, a thirty-five year old married man, and Francis Ellis, 22, were arraigned on a charge of violently and feloniously ravishing Martha Hawkesley, aged 16, at Beauchief. Baron Hullock presided at the trial, which followed the offence, on 19th March 1825.

Martha, and her fourteen year old sister, were returning from Sheffield. As they approached the Great Tom Cross field, the crime was perpetrated by Batty. Ellis took little part in the proceedings, merely preventing Martha from climbing over a stile in the field.

Batty went to Martha's house the next day to apologise, and try to put the matter right. He even fell to his knees and begged forgiveness, but Mr. Hawkesley would have none of it.

The Trial and Execu-  tion of GEORGE
BATTY, aged 36, at DERBY.

Who suffered Death this day, the 11th day of March, 1825, mitted a Rape on the Body of aged 16, at the Parish of Nor-

April 8, 1825, for having on violently assaulted, and com- Miss MARTHA HAWKESLEY, ton, in the County of Derby.

Miss Martha Hawkesley, onbe- box accompanied by her mo- ing woman; the young lady

ing called, entered the witness- ther, a respectable elderly look- appeared greatly agitated.

THE EXECUTION.

The time elapsed since his condemnation and this, to him, fatal morning, we are hap- py to learn, the unhappy man has employed in the most becoming manner, and earnest devotion. His wife and children have taken their last affectionate and affecting leave of him; and this forenoon, after receiving the blessed Sacrament, and going through the usual devotional exercises in the Chapel of the Prison, he was conducted to the fatal platform. When on the platform, and being tied up, he cast around him a wistful and lingering look on that scene of mortal existence, which, however reluctantly, he was about to quit for ever. The worthy Chaplain proceeded to read a selected part of the Burial Service, in which the unhappy man joined with great fervency; and as it was left to the Chaplain to give the fatal signal, he chose the precise moment when the dying criminal had these words in his mouth, " suffer us not at our last hour for any pains of death to fall from Thee," to give it--From Thee! vibrated on the ears of those around him; but to him it was the last vibration of the silver chord of life!--the bolt was drawn--the drop fell--and he was launched into eternity!

Extracts from a broadsheet, describing the execution of George Batty for rape in 1825. *Nottingham University Library*

At the trial Ellis was acquitted on the direction of the judge, and Batty was convicted and sentenced to death. Several witnesses for Batty had said that when he was drunk he could be truculent, but when sober he was a humane man.

The judge was very much affected by the sentence he had to pass, and halted three times before he could accomplish it.

George Batty was executed on 8th April.

Chapter III

THE VICTORIAN AGE

Victorian sentencing policy was very different from that exercised under the Bloody Code.

After a series of reforms instituted by Sir Robert Peel and John Russell in the 1830s, the use of the capital sentence was greatly restricted. In 1832, for example, the capital penalty was abolished for cattle, sheep and horse stealing. In 1833 it was abolished for housebreaking, in 1836 for forgery, and in 1837 for burglary.

By the early 1840s, capital punishment was only applicable for murder, attempted murder, high treason, rape, piracy with violence, and arson in Her Majesty's Dockyards. In practice, even this was misleading, for after 1841 only two people were executed for crimes other than murder. These cases, in 1851 and 1862, involved attempted murder.

In non-murder capital cases the judge would order the sentence of death to be recorded, rather than pronouncing it himself, and would then pass a lesser sentence on the malefactors.

There were utilitarian, as well as humanitarian, reasons for the liberalisation of the criminal law. The Bloody Code had proved ineffective because of the reluctance of jurymen to convict offenders in cases where they knew the death sentence would result. The substitution of imprisonment for capital punishment in theft cases resulted in higher conviction rates, and was thus a more effective deterrent than the draconian sentences that had hitherto existed.

Nineteenth century criminal statistics are unreliable indicators of actual crime levels, but murder is a highly visible, easily defined crime, so we can be fairly certain about its level of incidence, even allowing for the vagaries of the statistics.

What then was the pattern of murder in the nineteenth century?

The annual volumes of judicial statistics appear to show that murder and manslaughter reached a peak in the 1830s and 40s, and thereafter steadily declined. Some of this decline is probably due to the improvement in the economy which took place as the 'Hungry 40s' gave way to the comparative prosperity of the 1850s and 1860s. There were probably less murders committed out of desperation and hunger, during the course of robberies and burglaries, as unemployment fell. Certainly, few Derbyshire murders in the Victorian period appear to have been committed for economic gain.

The fall in murder and manslaughter may also owe something to the formation of the police forces, which replaced the old parish constables.

Sir Robert Peel's Metropolitan Police Act of 1829 had led to the formation of a trained police force in London. His example was soon followed in the provinces.

Derby had a borough police force in 1836, consisting of eleven men — one superintendent, two sergeants and eight constables. After stiff opposition from reluctant ratepayers, a Derbyshire County police force was constituted in 1857.

The impact they had on general crime levels is debatable, but their existence certainly made it much easier to mount immediate murder investigations, and to apprehend suspected murderers.

Forensic science was still in its infancy, so the police had no sophisticated aids such as fingerprints, or serum tests to help them in their investigations. They did, however, have the assistance of doctors and coroners, who compiled detailed reports containing such information as the angle a bullet entered a body, the injuries which actually caused death, and the presence or absence of poison in a corpse. These all helped to convict murderers in Victorian Derbyshire.

However the police did not solve all of the murders, and one of the most publicised of these was that involving Enoch Stone.

Enoch Stone, a silk glove maker who lived in Church

Street, Spondon, was returning home from Derby, where he had been to collect his washing, on 23rd June 1856.

He suffered from partial paralysis, and he had to walk slowly, burdened as he was with the clothes hamper and his crippled leg.

Enoch was last seen at about a quarter to eleven by the tollgate keeper on Nottingham Road. Two hours later, a servant employed by Mr. W. S. Cox, who was driving to Derby station to meet the mail train carrying his master, saw a hamper lying in the road with clothes strewn about it.

Further investigations revealed the figure of Enoch lying on his side. He was still alive but only just. He had been battered severely about the head with a heavy instrument. He was conveyed in the cart to his house, and a surgeon was summoned. But it was to no avail, for the unfortunate man expired at six o'clock that morning.

Over the next few days several suspicious characters were picked up, but all were eventually released due to lack of evidence.

There was a great public outrage that such an inoffensive man should have met with such a horrible fate, and the government offered £100 reward, a considerable sum of money at that time, and a full pardon to any person involved who had not actually perpetrated the murder.

But the reward was never claimed. The good citizens of Derby, however, were so touched by poor Enoch's demise that they organised a subscription to erect a memorial stone in his memory.

Eventually a small stone was erected near the site of the murder, bearing the initials 'E.S'. This can still be seen by the side of Nottingham Road, near its junction with Oregon Way.

The Memorial to Enoch on Nottingham Road, Chaddesden.
photograph: Philip Taylor

What sort of people did the

police apprehend for the crime of murder? One fact stands out above all others. The twenty-seven people convicted of murder in Derbyshire between 1837 and 1901 were overwhelmingly working class.

Only two were of a middle class background, George Townley and Gerald Mainwaring, and neither of them were Derbyshire people. The only other criminals with any claims to social superiority were George Smith, whose father owned four houses, although he himself was only a millhand, Anthony Turner, who had been employed as a debt collector, and Edward Wager, who was a tenant farmer.

The rest were working class; five were colliers, and the others included servants, sweeps, weavers, boatman and hawkers amongst their number.

Despite their poverty very few of them committed their murders for the purpose of financial gain. Only five of the twenty-four cases were committed to secure obvious pecuniary advantage. This would seem to confirm the opinion of Lord Romilly. Speaking in the House of Lords in 1866, Romilly said,

> "It should be borne in mind, that although murder was sometimes committed for the sake of plunder, yet in the great majority of cases plunder formed no part of the motive for commiting the crime".

However money, or rather lack of it, may have been the root cause of many murders carried out during the course of matrimonial disputes. This was by far the most common type of murder. Eight of the cases involved the murder of a woman by her husband, and one the murder of a man by his wife.

These wife murders were frequently just the culmination of years of brutal treatment by their men. Heavy drinking sessions were often the precursor to these outbreaks of homicidal violence.

Long hours of work, poor housing, and grinding poverty were not factors conducive to the promotion of domestic harmony, many men preferred to seek solace in the local taverns after their drudgery, rather than return to cold cheerless dwellings.

The Victorian working man certainly had no lack of choice when he came to select a place of refreshment, as the temperance movement often bitterly pointed out. In 1884, for example, Derby had no less than 233 public houses, 10 hotels, and 89 retailers of beer. Small wonder then that many men returned home to their wives inflamed by drink, and more than willing to react violently to any criticism of their behaviour. Heavy drinking played a significant part in no less than half of the 24 cases.

Sexual or emotional jealousy was also a significant element in many of the crimes. Two of our Victorian murderers killed their sweethearts after they had been rejected, and several of the husbands killed their wives because they suspected them of infidelity.

Another common Victorian crime was infanticide. The absence of effective methods of birth control led to many unwanted pregnancies. This problem was particularly acute for an unmarried woman. The birth of illegitimate children meant both social disgrace and economic hardship. In order to escape this situation some women resorted to desperate measures. Many women who killed their new born children escaped the death penalty, though, the jury preferring to bring in the alternative verdict of concealment of birth, as we shall see.

Another closely related offence was that of abortion. Anyone performing the operation itself was guilty of a felony, but if the recipient died that person was also tried for murder.

Murder committed for sexual motives appears only very infrequently in Assize calendars. This, however, may be misleading. It might well be the case that it was difficult to obtain convictions in such cases. Unlike the majority of murder cases, in which murderer and victim are known to each other, sex murders are usually committed indiscriminately. Unless the murderer confessed, therefore, or was caught in the act, he stood a good chance of escaping the consequences of his actions. There is only one definite example of such a murder during this period. Alfred Gough raped and then strangled a six year old girl in 1881. But there also appears to be a strong sexual element in the murder of

Ellen Wilkinson by John Wakefield in 1880. In this case rape had not occurred, but the prosecuting councel hinted that sexual assault could not be ruled out.

In both cases the villains were easily apprehended, for Wakefield had committed the murder in his own house, while wallpaper from Gough's handcart was found next to the little girl's body.

These people, then, are a representative cross-section of the type who appeared in the dock at Derby County Court in this period charged with the crime of murder.

After being apprehended by the police our Derbyshire murderers (or murderesses) had to devote some attention to the impending trial. Generally speaking, those arraigned were given a better trial than their eighteenth century counterparts, but the trials themselves exhibited features which would disturb a modern defence lawyer.

Murder trials are conducted meticulously, and often last several days, whereas the average Victorian murder trial tended to last a matter of hours. The Victorian prisoner also laboured under severe handicaps when conducting his defence. Until 1849, prisoners were not allowed to have a copy of the evidence against them, and until the introduction of the Criminal Evidence Act of 1898 they were not allowed to address the court.

Most were, however, adequately represented, for the very seriousness of the crime ensured that the offices of the best counsel available were procured. These cases often gave young barristers the opportunity to make a name for themselves. One of the most eminent nineteenth century judges, Sir James Fitzjames Stephen, started his career by defending prisoners at Derbyshire Assizes in the 1860s.

Stephen later became famous for his textbooks on criminal law, and for his advocacy of revision of the Criminal Code. His career, however, was to end on a tragic note. His handling of the Florence Maybrick poisoning case in 1889 caused a public outcry, which led to his retirement from the bench. Shortly afterwards, Stephen was confined to a mental home, where he subsequently died.

It was, however, one thing to get a prisoner into the dock,

quite another to convict him. One common defence plea was that of mental illness.

The rules governing mental illness as a mitigating factor in criminal acts were tightly drawn.

Provisions for such an occurrence were laid down by NcNaghten's rules. These stated that for a plea of insanity to be successful it had to be proved that,

> "At the time of committing the offence, the accused was labouring under such a defect of reason, from disease of the mind, as not to know the nature and quality of the act he was doing, or if he did know it, that he did not know that what he was doing was wrong".

This narrow interpretation meant that criminals who were mentally subnormal, suffering from schizophrenia, or under such stress that they were incapable of controlling their behaviour, were still liable to the capital penalty as long as they could understand that murder was wrong.

Poor Daniel Freeman, for example, killed Sarah Webb of Sawley in 1852, by striking her head with a stone, and then, incongruously, with a tea tray and a clock. At his trial, a policeman reported that he had found Freeman wandering around in a state of nudity, picking particles of food from a dung heap.

The judge, Mr. Justice Coleridge, guided by McNaghten's rules, sentenced the poor man to death, although he was subsequently reprieved, and placed in an asylum.

Despite the fact that judges strictly adhered to McNaghten's guidelines, many defence lawyers continued to use the argument of mental illness to try to save their clients from the gallows.

Although the death penalty was now only applicable to murder, there were still often a great reluctance on the part of juries to convict because of the nature of the penalty.

They might be persuaded to bring in a verdict of manslaughter instead, a verdict some judges believed to be not always supported by the facts.

Lord Abinger, for example, stated at the trial of Henry

Hoskisson for the murder of the Earl of Chesterfield's gamekeeper in 1841, that

> "The jury had given the prisoner the benefit of the doubt, but he could not help thinking that he shot the deceased deliberately, without any violence being offered by the latter. It was quite clear from the expressions he used, that he went out with the determination to resist any attempt that might be made to apprehend him, and that he had never met with a case that called for a more severe punishment than his".

Similarly Baron Parke said of the acquittal of Harry Spencer for the murder of John Pidcock at the Swan Inn in Ashbourne, that

> "The jury had taken a most lenient view of the case. He was bound by his oath to tell them that he did not see any circumstances that would mitigate, and reduce the crime from murder to manslaughter, and had they acted on his direction he, the prisoner, would be standing a convicted murderer, and receiving the sentence of death".

There existed, then, a strong possibility that the accused could avoid the death penalty.

Even if convicted, it was by no means certain that he would be executed. If the jury did find the prisoner guilty they could often find extenuating circumstances such as youth, or lack of premeditation in the commission of the crime. They could than add a strong recommendation for mercy, which the judge would forward to the Home Secretary.

Those murderers who were reprieved were sentenced to penal servitude for life. This expression requires some explanation.

In the early nineteenth century, criminals committing serious crimes had either been executed or transported to one of His Majesty's colonies. The diminution of the capital penalty, and the ending of transportation in the 1860s, resulted in the authorities being left with a large surplus of criminals on their hands.

Their solution to the problem was to build more prisons, and institute penal servitude. A harsh prison regime was introduced, designed to make life so unpleasant that an offender would never wish to come back.

The liberal use of the treadmill, both as a means of exercise and as punishment, was a common sight in nineteenth century prisons. A man working a treadmill could expect to 'climb' the equivalent of 7,500 feet a day. In the cells, a handcrank fixed to the wall, set at 12lbs pressure, had to be turned by a villain as much as 10,000 revolutions a day. In the exercise yard he might be instructed to take part in shot drill. This involved lifting 24lb cannon balls above the head for a period of some 75 minutes.

This regime could be relied upon to break the spirit of all but the most hardened criminals. However, prison sentences were reduced for good behaviour. Prisoners were also allowed out on parole. But if they committed any crime whilst out, they could be brought back to serve the rest of the original sentence. These convicts, nicknamed 'ticket of leave' men were the subject of much controversy in the nineteenth century.

Prisoners sentenced to life imprisonment were subject to the same rules as other offenders.

It is fashionable to contrast the 'life sentences' passed today, which result on average in murderers serving about nine years, with the good old days when a life sentence meant just that. But 'life' never meant life, even in Victorian Britain. Few Victorian prisoners served more than twenty years and most served considerably less.

The idea that the Victorians were prolific hangers is another myth that can easily be dispelled.

In 1870, for example, of 101 cases reported to the police as murder, only 41 resulted in an indictment for this crime. Of these 41 persons, some were cleared of the crime altogether, and others were convicted of manslaughter only. 15 people were convicted of murder and sentenced to death, but only 6 of them were actually executed. The following year, 13 people were sentenced to death, and 4 executed.

Derbyshire figures show that of the 28 people sentenced to

death between 1843 and 1901, in itself not an exceptional number, 15 were executed and 13 were reprieved. National figures reveal that in the years 1840 to 1900, the reprieve for men varied between 42.6% and 48% of those convicted.

Thus execution was by no means a foregone conclusion for anyone convicted of murder. Sex and social class were factors which seem to have had a strong influence on whether those convicted suffered the death penalty. Of the 665 people executed between 1843 and 1900, only 50 were women.

It is true, of course, that women committed fewer murders than men, but it is also true that women received a more sympathetic hearing from the judge and jury when they found themselves in court faced with death. Many women were undoubtedly acquitted because of their sex.

Even if a woman was convicted she stood a good chance of escaping execution. 199 women were sentenced to death between 1843 and 1900, but in only 50 of the cases was the sentence actually carried out. All of the four Derbyshire women convicted of murder in this period had their sentences commuted to life imprisonment.

It is also the case that women convicted of the killing of their new born children were hardly ever sentenced to death, even though the law made no distinction between the death of a baby and an adult. A random sample of Derbyshire Assize cases between 1837 and 1860 show that the jury took a comparatively lenient view of this crime. Of the 19 cases in which a woman was charged with the wilful murder of an infant child, in only one was a conviction actually obtained. The other women were found guilty of the much less serious crime of concealment of birth. This was punishable by a prison sentence of from three months to two years. Sometimes it is obvious that the mother was guilty.

At the trial of Hannah Slack in 1844, Dr. Evans stated that he had not the slightest doubt that the child had died from taking arsenic, but the jury said that Hannah was a good mother and acquitted her.

In March 1850 Elizabeth Vicar's new born child was found with a tape tied tightly around its neck. The jury found Elizabeth guilty of concealment of birth, and Judge Platt agreed, sentencing her to one years imprisonment.

Social class could also play a part in evasion of the gallows for both men and women.

The most celebrated Victorian murder cases all involved middle class people. Drs. Smethurst, Palmer and Lamson received star billing for their crimes, while such pillars of Victorian women's society as Florence Bravo, Madelaine Smith and Florence Maybrick achieved national prominence as a result of their court appearences. All, incidentally, used poison as the agent of death.

It was, of course, the very fact that the rich and respectable found themselves in the dock on a charge of murder that made their cases *cause celebres* in the first place. Wealth and social status were obvious advantages once the accused was brought to court.

Money could procure the best barristers and legal counsel available. It was even possible to hire government officers, up to the rank of Attorney-General, to defend oneself.

If the accused was found guilty it was also easy to find influential men to put their signatures on petitions to be sent to the Home Secretary for a reprieve. Eminent medical men, such as Dr. Forbes Winslow would be prevailed upon to plead mental instability as a mitigating circumstance.

It was widely believed by the working classes that many middle class murderers escaped the ultimate penalty for their crimes because of their social status.

The London crowds who gathered to watch the execution of Thomas Wright for the murder of his wife during a domestic dispute certainly thought so. Over one thousand police had to be drafted in to control a crowd who shouted 'Shame', 'Judicial murder' and 'Where's Townley?'. The Mainwaring case also brought out the class bias inherent in Victorian murder cases. Mainwaring, a wealthy playboy, had the Solicitor-General to represent him, and was to escape the scaffold with a life sentence.

But judges could also on occasion take surprisingly liberal stands on cases with which we might have expected them to have little sympathy.

In 1854, William Bagshawe, a wealthy Derbyshire landowner, who lived at Wormhill Hall, was killed during a battle with trout poachers on the River Wye, near Miller's Dale. The poachers were indicted for murder, but after hearing the evidence Justice Maule spoke up favourably for the poachers, and criticised Bagshawe's party for taking the law into their own hands.

Maule pointed out first of all that the jury should know that in this case even if there had been no intention to take life deliberately, the law made the crime murder because any death incurred during a felony, whether deliberate or accidental, was held to be constructive murder, and was punishable by the death penalty. However Maule went on to say that,

> "He could not find that anyone of Bagshawe's party spoke to being struck before they struck themselves, and the poachers might well consider they were attacked in a very violent way.
> If anything had been said by Mr. Bagshawe's party that they should apprehend the poachers, that would have been complete notice, but it did not follow that such notice was absolutely required. It was curious, however, that no word should be uttered by the watchers of their intention to take the men into custody.
> In the absence of any intimation being given Taylor (one of the poachers) came out of the water and gave himself up, and it was possible that the others might have done so as well, if they had been called upon".

The jury promptly acquitted the poachers. The decision outraged many of the prominent men of Derbyshire, and a flood of letters was sent to the local papers complaining about the decision. Some of them felt that an unfortunate precedent might have been set creating a 'poachers charter' that would prevent the apprehension of such men. The decision does, however, suggest that the judiciary were willing to examine the facts of the case, rather than yielding to pressure from the local squirearchy.

Nor were Victorian judges without a sense of humour, albeit of a black kind.

It was in an 1860 Derbyshire bigamy case that the accused plaintively asked,

> "Will your Lordship allow me to speak to the congregation?"

Justice Williams, giving the culprit a withering look, replied,

> "Certainly not, you are not a clergyman".

Victorian barristers also seem to have had their share of humorous experiences. Robert Walton wrote down some of his in a book entitled *'Random Recollections of the Midland Circuit'*, in 1869. Walton states that,

> "Derbyshire common juries in former times, were not held in much estimation, though they are now as good, probably, as the average lot of jurymen, but some of the verdicts they returned were curious specimens of the wisdom of jurymen. It was in some petty larceny cases that a Derbyshire jury acquitted the accused, recommending his lordship to tell him, 'not to do it again!"

In another case, a man was accused of murdering his wife by beating her to death with a poker.

> "In the course of the evidence, it came out that the deceased was of an aggravating temper, one of the daughter's of Eve who are always nagging at their husbands. Under these circumstances, the jury returned a verdict of 'Served her just right'".

Once convicted, a nineteenth century murderer would usually appeal to the Home Secretary for a commutation of sentence. The Home Secretary, acting on behalf of the Monarch, was empowered to bestow the prerogative of mercy, and he alone, unlike eighteenth century judges, had the power to decide who should hang and who should not.

The judges could put forward their own recommendations for clemency, and it would appear that this carried more weight than the juries plea for mercy, but the Home Secretary took the ultimate decision.

If the decision to reprieve was not forthcoming, the condemned prisoners were hanged on the New Drop at the County Gaol in Vernon Street.

The experience of a public execution was supposed to impress on the spectators the punishment which would inevitably be inflicted on those who committed the dreadful crime of murder. It was also to allay working class suspicions. They feared that the rich and influential would be able to escape punishment if executions were privately conducted.

Far from the execution being seen as a salutary lesson which would instill a reverence for the due processes of law into those viewing the scene, the executions often assumed the air of a festival, and general levity was exhibited. Stalls selling hot potatoes, lemonade, and songsheets did a roaring trade. Charles Dickens was only being slightly ironical when he placed in *Household Words* an account of the hanging of Mrs. French of Lewes in 1852 under the heading of 'Open Air Entertainments'.

Special trains were laid on to take people to the executions, while those who lived in the neighbourhood would often walk miles to see the last acts of the drama. The affluent gallows-watchers would even hire rooms overlooking the scaffold in order to get a good view of the wretched criminal's last moments. The *Mercury* records the scene of the execution of Bonsall, Bland and Hulme as follows.

> "The concourse of persons was by far greater than on any similar occasion in Derby. The crowd, as seen from the scaffold presented a densely packed mass of human beings covering the whole spacious area in front of the prison, and extending through the whole of Vernon Street and into Friargate. The roads, gardens, yards, windows, housetops, in fact every possible situation commanding a view of the drop had its separate crowd of gazers".

It is estimated that 50,000 people attended this execution. A truly staggering figure when it is remembered that the whole population of Derby at this time numbered only about 38,000. The executions of Platts and Smith were each believed to have attracted crowds of 20,000 people.

Interest was so great that broadsheets carrying the details of the murder, trial, and confessions of the unfortunate person were sold in their thousands on the day of the execution. It is estimated that two and a half million broadsheets were sold about the murder for which the Mannings suffered in 1849.

Executions were also the occasion for proselytising by religious organisations. The drama of the spectacle could be employed to pressure the more impressionable amongst the crowd to make instant religious commitments. The *Derby Mercury* reports that 13,000 religious tracts were distributed amongst the crowd at the execution of Platts in 1847.

The morbid interest lasted well into the nineteenth century, long after public executions had been abolished. Large crowds would gather at prisons on the day of the execution to see the raising of the Black Flag, which denoted that an execution was taking place, the tolling of the bell, and to read the notice of execution pinned to the door of the prison.

By the early twentieth century, however, changing social attitudes, coupled with the sweeping away of the last rituals associated with executions, the black flag and the bell, killed the sense of drama attached to the occasion. Only a few hundred people were reported as attending the execution of John Silk in 1906.

The chief executioner throughout most of the early Victorian period was William Calcraft. Calcraft 'reigned' from 1829-1874. He appears to have been a particularly inept hangman. Eighteenth century victims had often suffered from slow strangulation, but nineteenth century criminals, in theory, were expected to die instantly when the trap-door was released on the scaffold. Calcraft's patients, however, were often denied such a merciful fate, and many were throttled as a result of his incompetence.

William Marwood, who succeeded Calcraft in 1874, approached his task more scientifically. Marwood drew up a table of weights and heights of his customers, which he believed would enable him to successfully calculate the exact length of rope needed to secure an instantaneous death of them.

Marwood's second execution was that of Benjamin

Hudson, the West Handley wife murderer. This went off with little difficulty.

Marwood's successor was James Berry. Berry did not return the hangman's craft to the days of Calcraft, but he was guilty of some technical blunders. So many, in fact, that a Select Committee of the House of Lords, chaired by Lord Aberdare, was appointed to look into the situation in 1888.

Fortunately Derby's executions appear to have exhibited none of these unsavoury features, though there is some evidence that death did not always come instantly to the hangman's victims. Of Platt's execution, for example, it was remarked,

> "He suffered much for a short time".

while of George Smith's end it was reported,

> "He dropped about four yards, and appeared to die instantly, but to those nearest the scaffold it could be seen that there was a muscular movement going on for about ten minutes, before life had become quite extinct".

This was the fate in store for those unfortunate enough to be convicted of murder at the County Hall in Derby, who were unable to escape the awful sentence of the law.

Convictions for Murder in Derbyshire 1837-1882

Samual Bonsall, William Bland and John Hulme for the murder of Martha Goddard at Stanley Hall.
Executed 31st March 1843.

John Platts for the murder of George Collis at Chesterfield.
Executed 1st April 1847.

Anthony Turner for the murder of Phoebe Barnes at Belper.
Executed 26th March 1852.

Daniel Freeman for the murder of Sarah Webb.
Sentenced Commuted: transferred to a lunatic asylum in June 1852.

George Smith for the murder of his father Joseph Smith at Ilkeston.
Executed 16th August 1861.

Richard Thorley for the murder of Eliza Morrow at Derby.
Executed 11th April 1862.

George Victor Townley for the murder of Bessie Goodwin, his sweetheart, at Wigwell Grange.
Sentence commuted to life imprisonment.

James Potter for the murder of Sarah Potter, his wife, at Derby.
Sentence commuted: transferred to Broadmoor Lunatic Asylum, March 1865.

Edward Wager for the murder of Harriet Wager, his wife, at Great Longstone.
Sentence commuted to life imprisonment, March 1867.

Samuel Wallis for the murder of Sarah Wallis, his wife, at Chesterfield.
Sentence commuted: transferred to Broadmoor, December 1871.

Benjamin Hudson for the murder of Eliza Hudson at West Handley.
Executed 4th August 1873.

Rose Brown for the murder of William Brown, her husband, at Derby.
Sentence commuted to life imprisonment, July 1875.

Gerald Mainwaring for the murder of P.C. Moss at Derby.
Sentence commuted to life imprisonment, August 1879.

Thomas Spooner Litherland for the murder of Sarah Litherland, his wife, at Winshill, near Burton.
Sentence commuted: transferred to Broadmoor, August 1879.

John Wakefield for the murder of Ellen Wilkinson at Derby.
Executed 16th August 1880.

Mary Wright for the murder of Adeline Wright, her daughter, at Bonsall.
Sentence commuted to life imprisonment, August 1880.

Albert Robinson for the murder of Jane Robinson, his wife, at Hadfield.
Executed 28th February 1881.

Alfred Gough for the murder of Eleanor Windle at Brimington.
Executed 21st November 1881.

Chapter IV

MURDER MOST FOUL

The Stanley Hall Murder

Early in the morning of Friday 30th September, 1842, William Scattergood, a farmer living near Stanley was awakened by a furious knocking. Surprised at being so rudely disturbed, Scattergood threw open the window to see who had the impertinence to awake him at such a time. He was even more surprised when he recognised his nocturnal visitor, as being Sarah Goddard.

Sarah and her sister Martha lived about a hundred yards distant, at isolated Stanley Hall. The two elderly ladies were recluses to such a degree that they refused to eat their meals together, or even have any servants living on the premises.

Their eccentricity made the house a tempting proposition to prospective burglars, and it had already been burgled twice that year. After the last occurrence anxious friends had begged the Misses Goddard to allow them to send menservants to sleep in the house, but they had both been emphatic in their rejection of this idea. Now it began to look as if they might be in trouble. Scattergood dressed quickly and followed Sarah back to the Hall. When he arrived he found her in the kitchen nursing a badly gashed head, and a broken finger. She was understandably in a state of shock, and Scattergood could only extract from her a garbled story about a burglary.

Fearing for the safety of Martha Goddard, Scattergood ran upstairs and entered her bedroom. There he encountered a dreadful sight.

Martha lay stretched on the bed. Her skull had been fractured by two or three heavy blows to the head.

Stanley Hall today. *photograph: Philip Taylor*

William saw that she was still alive, and called in Dr. Bowden. Bowden examined Martha, but there was little he could do for her, and she expired within half an hour of his visit.

A man-hunt was started immediately and it soon brought rewards.

From the beginning the three most obvious suspects were John Hulme, a sweep, and two colliers, Samuel Bonsall and William Bland. These three men lived within a hundred yards of each other in the village of Heage.

Joseph Simpson, a needlemaker, believed that John Hulme, his next door neighbour, was involved in the burglary. He interrogated Hulme, telling him he was a suspect in the Stanley murder case, but Hulme denied any knowledge of the crime. Simpson, however, was not convinced, and possibly motivated by the thought of a reward he decided to go in search of Richard Dronfield, Hulme's apprentice.

He found Dronfield on his chimney cleaning round near Idridgehay, and questioned him about Hulme's movements. Dronfield had an interesting story to tell. On the morning of the murder he remembered Hulme and Bonsall returning to the cottage with several articles of women's clothing. Later

Bland joined them, and they agreed to hide the clothes until things quietened down. Then Dronfield took Simpson to a sough near Ambergate, where several articles were recovered.

Simpson called on John Hawkins, the parish constable of Heage. Hawkins searched the homes of Bonsall and Bland, and found other articles of clothing. The pair were taken into custody on 4th October.

Hulme, who had been tipped off about the arrest of his associates, had fled to his mother's house in Leek, and from thence to nearby Marstons Wood. After a few days he made inquiry of his mother whether the coast was clear, but she went straight to the local constable, and Hulme was apprehended.

The trial of the three men took place before Mr. Baron Gurney on 26th March 1843. Sergeant Clarke, Mr. Whitehurst and Mr. Fowler prosecuted. Mr. Miller defended Bonsall, who was the only one of the three to employ counsel.

The fact that the three men had in their possession articles of clothing from Stanley Hall established their guilt from the outset. The three defendants, therefore, individually tried to persuade the court that although they had been present at the burglary, they had not been the person who perpetrated the actual murder. Both Bland and Hulme signed depositions stating that Bonsall had struck the fatal blows with a crow bar. Bonsall contradicted this claiming that Bland had struck the fatal blow.

The three men realised they would be convicted of the crime, but hoped by claiming that they were merely accomplices of the murderer to escape the supreme penalty of the law.

A disturbing feature of this case appears to be the fact that

> "a promise of pardon was made to any accomplice, except the one who actually committed the murder".

This offer was made before the statements of Bland and Hulme were taken, according to Mr. Hutchinson, the clerk to the magistrates.

The defence could offer little assistance to the accused. It was difficult to counter the overwhelming evidence against them.

Joseph Roe, a farmer, testified to meeting the men on the road from Stanley to Heage at half past two in the morning. Suspecting them of poaching, he asked them what they had in their bags, and they had threatened him with violence.

William Salt and John Brown, who not only shared a cell with Bonsall but also his bed (a fact which speaks volumes about early nineteenth century prison conditions), testified that Bonsall had admitted his guilt to them.

Most damning of all was the testimony of Dronfield, who witnessed the division of the spoils.

Mr. Miller, defending Bonsall, tried vainly to persuade the jury that the evidence of the witnesses was suspect.

It was to no avail. The jury took only ten minutes to reach its verdict of guilty. Baron Gurney said,

> "I consider the guilt of all three of you as one, and the same. The sentence of the court is that you be taken to the place whence you came, and from thence to a place of execution, and that you be severally hanged until you are dead, and your bodies buried within the precincts of the gaol. And may God Almighty have mercy on your guilty souls".

At which Bonsall retorted,

> "There is no God".

The date for their execution was fixed as 31st March.

Whilst awaiting execution, the men confessed that this was not their first crime. Bonsall and Hulme had previously robbed Mr. Fletcher of Pentrich on the Queen's Highway, and had broken into the same gentlemans mill, for the purpose of plundering it.

Bonsall and Bland cited Hulme as the ringleader, and blamed him for their current predicament. His occupation as a sweep had made an ideal cover for scouting out houses for potential burglary. This he seems to have done with some success, although he might have been wise to take heed of the fate of two of his brothers, who had both been transported.

When all hope of a reprieve had gone, Bonsall admitted that he had inflicted on Martha Goddard the fatal injuries, but stressed that the others had also beaten and ill-used her.

A broadsheet describing the trial and execution of the Heage men in 1843
Nottingham University Library

Portraits of Bonsall, Bland and Hulme from the *Derby and Chesterfield Reporter*
Derby Central Library, Local Studies Department

The crowd at their execution on 31st March 1843, was enormous. Both the *Mercury* and the *Reporter* put the number at between forty and fifty thousand people. The fact that the execution was a triple affair, falling on the day of Easter Fair, when more people than usual were in the town probably accounts for this phenomenon.

The executioner was Haywood of Appleby, and he seems to have carried off the executions with some degree of competence, for we are told that,

> "Bonsall died instantly, and that the bodily sufferings of Hulme and Bland were of brief duration".

Bonsall continued to pray fervently until the drop fell, crying out, "Lord have mercy upon me, Christ have Mercy".

After the execution, the crowd dispersed, many returning to outlying towns such as Chesterfield and Belper, on the special trains laid on for the executions. Here the self-control and decorum apparently present at the execution was abandoned, and we are told by the *Reporter* that,

> "So great was the rush to get off by the first train that it was with great difficulty the crowd could be restrained by closing the doors. A very disgraceful scene ensued, fighting, wrestling, swearing etc. as fifteen hundred people, many of them intoxicated, were sent off by the two special trains".

Butchery in the Shambles

On a cold December night in 1845, John Heathcote, a joiner, was returning from an Oddfellows meeting at the Peacock Inn in Chesterfield, when he was confronted by a strange sight.

Three men were carrying a large bundle from a butcher's shop in the Shambles, across Low Pavement, and into a narrow lane known as Buntings Yard. Two men emerged from the yard later, but this time without their bundle.

Heathcote, who was accompanied by his brother Godfrey,

was intrigued by this singular occurrence, but soon forgot all about it. The full significance of this was to be brought home to him later, however, when on 28 August 1846, workmen clearing out the nightsoil and manure from the cesspit in Buntings Yard dug up what they took to be the carcass of a sheep. A later examination showed it to be a man.

The shreds of clothing still attached to the skeleton pointed to the body being that of George Collis, who had mysteriously disappeared the previous December.

Collis, who was 26 at the time he vanished, was a former servant who had entered into partnership with John Platts. The pair had carried on a butchery business in the Shambles, in a shop belonging to George Parker. Collis had put up the capital for their joint venture, while Platts had brought his experience of the trade into the partnership.

Several people had questioned Platts about Collis' disappearence, but Platts had maintained that Collis had run off to Manchester owing him money.

At the coroner's inquest on 3rd September, suspicion again centred on Platts. Several witnesses testified to having seen him and another butcher, George Morley, behaving suspiciously on the night Collis disappeared. Constable Shore had searched Platts' house a few weeks before, suspecting him of thefts from his previous employer, Mr. Statham. He had found nothing, but he now recollected that he had seen a yellow purse and a pawn ticket for a watch. Thinking that they may have some bearing on the case, Sharpe returned to the house, but the ticket and purse had gone.

It was later revealed that Platts' mother had redeemed the watch, and Platts gave instructions to the police so it could be recovered. He claimed that he had purchased the watch from a character known as Lanky Bill, who kept a house of ill repute in Chesterfield. But the watch was identified by the watchmaker as belonging to George Collis, so Platts was committed to the County Gaol, to await the arrival of the Assizes Judge.

The trial excited tremendous interest, and crowds fought to get into the County Hall in St. Mary's Gate. Mr. Justice

Patterson presided over the trial on 19th March. Mr Humfrey presented the case for the Crown, and Mr. Macaulay defended Platts. Platts took his trial alone because the other two men suspected of involvement in Collis' murder were not available to attend.

George Morley had, with a fine sense of drama, died of typhus two days after the inquest, while the third person involved was not known to the authorities at this time.

The case against Platts was entirely circumstantial, the most damaging fact being his possession of several articles known to have been worn by Collis on the night of his disappearance.

Much play was made by the prosecution that Platts had been seen by a group of people, Thomas and Elizabeth Harvey, Elizabeth's sister, Phoebe Bellamy, and her husband Thomas, in his shop on the night in question, and that sounds of violence had emanated from it.

The Heathcote brothers testified to seeing Platts, Morley and Collis together in Morley's shop on the Sunday, and spoke about the curious procession they had seen going up Buntings Yard the following night.

Mr. Macaulay tried to persuade the jury that the witnesses were not recalling what had actually happened on the fateful night sixteen months previously, but what they had read in the Chesterfield papers since, which had 'refreshed' their memories.

However, this plausible line of attack received a severe mauling when many of the witnesses revealed that they could not read.

To the argument that the witnesses could not be expected to remember one particular night in December from others after such a long time, the prosecution could provide evidence that the Harveys' and Bellamys' were absolutely certain of the night in question, because they were celebrating the wedding of a neighbour. The registry office entry was produced which showed beyond any doubt that the night was 7 December 1845, the night Collis had disappeared.

In his summing up for the defence, Mr. Macaulay attempted to persuade the jury that a case of *corpus delicti* had not been proven. How, for example, did they know that the body was that of Collis? The evidence, he said, was minimal.

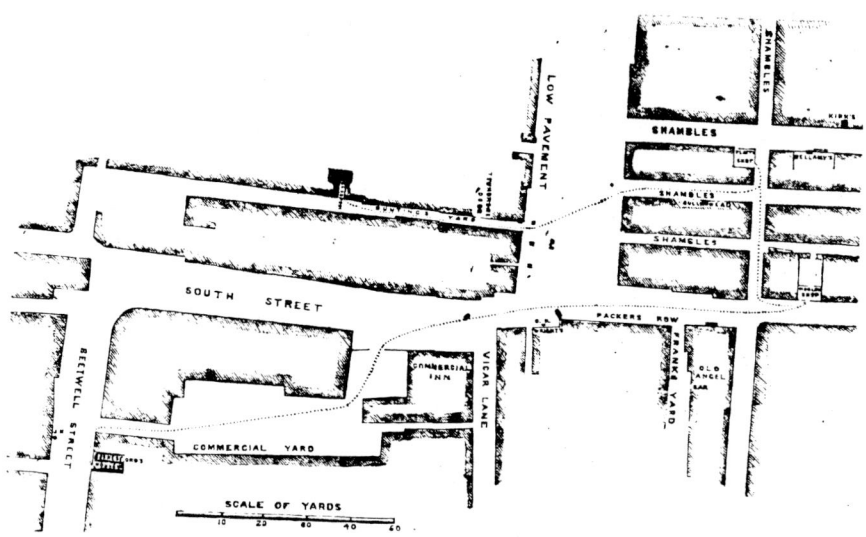

Plan of the Shambles in Chesterfield showing the path taken by Platts when disposing of the body of George Collis.

Derby Central Library Local Studies Department

By this time the trial had been going on for so long, the time being past 10.30 at night, that the judge ordered the jury home, with instructions to appear the following morning. The next day, after considering their verdict, the jury announced that they found Platts guilty of the wilful murder of George Collis.

Platts appeared to accept his fate philosophically, blaming Morley for his situation.

In his confession Platts says that the murder took place neither in his shop or Morley's, but in a stable. Morley and Launt (the *Reporter* omits this last name for obvious reasons) were the other people involved in the murder. Platts stated that,

> "Morley was to strike the blow, because he was the strongest man, and Launt and I were to assist in strangling him".

This last statement has the ring of truth about it, because Platts was only 4' 11" high.

His execution took place on 1 April, before a crowd of twenty thousand. Haywood was the executioner, and although the hanging was successful, Platts

> "struggled, his hands and left arm were seen to move to and fro as far as his irons would allow for nearly two minutes, when all motion ceased".

The *Reporter* criticised the tendency in certain quarters to regard Platts as a sort of hero. The defects in his character, it said, were traceable to his antecedents. It was a

> "lamentable fact that he was not only an illegitimate child himself, but that he became a father of a child only three weeks since, by a girl with whom he cohabited".

In a postscript to the Collis murder, Anthony Launt, the third man, was arraigned for the murder of George Collis at the August Assizes in 1847. He was acquitted after a short trial.

The Deadly Dispute at Belper

Anthony Turner, a tailor, was employed as a rent collector by a Mr. Walker, who owned property in Belper and lived at Field House in that town. He had also agreed to bring up an illegitimate child of Walker's, for which service he and his wife received a sum of money.

In April 1851 Mr. Walker died and his estate passed to Mrs. Phoebe Barnes, Walker's sister. Turner continued to act as a rent collector on behalf of Mrs. Barnes, but when he broached the subject of maintenance for the child, Mrs. Barnes not only refused to accept any responsibility but implied that the child was Turner's.

The dispute continued, and getting no satisfaction Turner deducted the amount due to him for the child from Mrs. Barnes' rents. She summoned him to a meeting at Field House. The interview developed into a full scale row, during which Mrs. Barnes apparently told Turner she would never pay a shilling for the child. Turner replied by picking up the inkstand, saying

> "you have no more religion in your heart than that, or you would not say so".

Mrs. Barnes requested that Turner surrender all his bills to her for auditing, and Turner stormed out of the house.

On 27th December 1851, Mrs. Barnes sent Turner the following letter.

Dec 27, 1851

Mr. Anthony Turner, Belper Lane End.

> Not being satisfied with your proceedings I do hereby give you notice that I have authorised and appointed Mr. John Bridges to collect and receive my rents in your place, and I do by this notice discharge you from collecting or receiving any more of my rents, wherever or whatsoever, from this 27 day of December, eighteen hundred and fifty one. As witness my hand.

This letter had the effect of completely unbalancing Turner. In his misery he turned to drink, a course of action out of keeping with his known habits.

In this volatile state he turned up at the house of John Haslam, a chemist at Belper Lane End, at eight o'clock at night. Haslam and his wife saw that Anthony was agitated and asked him to sit down and have a smoke. Turner showed them the letter, and then, his emotions getting the better of him, he cried

> "I think I shall do something to be talked of"

and ran off taking a knife from the shop with him. Haslam called after him, but Turner refused to return.

Suspecting that Turner intended to harm Mrs. Barnes, Haslam got his hat and coat and swiftly followed, but he was too late to prevent the tragedy that followed.

Mrs. Barnes cook, Harriet Storer answered the door in response to Turner's frenzied knockings. Noting the wildness in his eyes, Harriet ushered him into the kitchen. She told

Mrs. Barnes that Turner wanted to see her, and warned her that he was drunk. Phoebe Barnes took the hint and bolted the sitting room door as a precaution.

Harriet returned to the kitchen and tried to persuade Anthony to leave, but he pushed her aside and ran upstairs. When Phoebe refused him admission to her room, he kicked down the door.

The Rev. Bannister, a relation of Mrs. Barnes, was alerted by Harriet, and ran upstairs to help. He found Turner standing over Mrs. Barnes. Her throat had been cut from ear to ear, and she died two minutes later.

Bannister did not realise the seriousness of Phoebe's injuries because he was extremely short-sighted, so he simply ushered Turner out of the room. Going downstairs Turner saw Harriet in the act of sending for the constables. He slashed at her face with his knife, fortunately missing her but severing one of her cap 'whiskers'. Turner chased her into the breakfast room, and would probably have added a second murder to his first if the alarm bell at the house had not suddenly started to ring.

He ran off onto the Chesterfield road, and wandered round in a trance for several days, finally returning to Belper on the Monday night. There he was seen in Belper Lane End, and took refuge at the cottage of Mrs. Spencer. Two Belper constables, Messrs. Wragg and Taylor, went to the cottage to arrest Turner, whereupon he attempted to cut his own throat.

Turner took his trial on 13 March 1852. Mr. Hayes and Mr. Balguy Jr. prosecuted, while Mr. Adams defended Turner.

The decision of the jury was never in doubt. Adams' tactic was to try and persuade the jury that the case was one of manslaughter, that

> "In a moment of ungovernable passion, having had recourse to that wretched, intoxicating drink, to which it is clear that he had resorted, he in that state committed the deed".

But the jury found him guilty, and he was sentenced to death.

Turner's plight aroused a great deal of sympathy. The provocation that he had received, and the fact that he had no previous criminal record carried some weight with the good citizens of Derby and Belper. Indeed, prior to the crime Turner had led a life of respectability. An indifferent and enthusiastic tailor by trade, he had previously been a Sunday School teacher at Shottle, and was for many years an agent of the Conservative party in South Derbyshire. His confession reveals him to be a man of some education.

A deputation was despatched to the Home Secretary, Spencer Walpole, which included Derby's two M.P.s, Michael Bass and Thomas Heyworth. They carried with them a petition signed by four thousand people urging clemency. But the Home Secretary refused to stop the execution, and so Anthony Turner was hanged on 26th March by William Calcraft.

The crowd was estimated at between fifteen and twenty thousand. The *Reporter* regrets that

> "A large proportion of the spectators consisted of women and children, the women especially being very numerous. We also noticed a great number of females with babes at the breast. One woman in Vernon Street had no less than eight small children with her. They were all dressed up for the occasion, and no doubt she thought she was giving them an intellectual treat. Indeed the scene resembled a pleasure fair more than anything else".

The Greyhound Stadium, Vernon Street, Derby, once the County Prison. Scene of the executions of nineteenth century murderers, including that of Anthony Turner. *photograph: Philip Taylor*

'Here's A Heart That Ne'er Will Fail'

Bath Street, Ilkeston, was in an uproar on the night of 1 May 1861, as seventeen year old Henry Smith and his younger brother Edward woke their sister Sarah, who also lived in the Street, with cries of murder. Hurrying next door with their neighbour Isaac Aldred, they found the boys' father, Joseph Smith, lying across the floor with a gaping hole in the back of his head.

Shortly afterwards, Joseph's eldest son George arrived at the house with a friend, Reuben Davis, and immediately became the prime suspect for the murder of his father.

Joseph Smith had been a man of some substance, owning four houses in Bath Street, and having a sum of £144 deposited in Nottingham Savings Bank. Joseph enjoyed cordial relations with his two younger sons, but the same cannot be said to have applied to George, of whom he despaired.

George Smith, aged 20 at the time of his trial, was a millhand employed by Ball and Co., lacemakers, of Ilkeston. He appears to have had little enthusiasm for his chosen profession, preferring to spend his days carousing in the public houses of Ilkeston, and as the *Reporter* would have it,

> "He was seen in the streets with a cigar in his mouth, was seen with the harlot, and the low theatres, which so often frequent the town of Ilkeston, were his element".

The adoption of this lifestyle was bound to have repercussions eventually, and in April 1861 George made a girl called Ellen Smith pregnant.

Smith had a genuine affection for the girl, and desparate for money he approached his father for help, but was brusquely rejected. In a note of despondency, Smith started to contemplate desperate measures. He wrote to Ellen on 29th April.

> "My Dear, I told my father this morning, and he is like a madman, and I am sure that he will make

away with himself, but Ellen never mind you will soon become my wife, and then all this bother will be over. Please send me word when you are at your Grandmothers, and you must come and meet me at the station on Sunday morning, be there at eight o'clock. So good by my Sweet Art. I have given the Banes in at Ilkeston".

The reference to his father 'making away' with himself was to assume more significance later, in view of what occurred.

George seems to have persuaded himself that if his father were to die his financial embarrassments would be swiftly resolved. Two workmates, Bell and Ellis, were to testify at the trial that he had approached them to enquire what his position would be if his father died intestate.

On the day of the murder George went to Nottingham, accompanied by Henry Davis, Reuben's brother, and his father's bank book. George tried to withdraw fourteen pounds from the Savings Bank, but the manager refused, pointing out that he had no authority to endorse such a transaction.

Smith approached a wine and spirit dealer called Bridger, with whom he had had previous dealings. Bridger lent him a sovereign on account, retaining the passbook as security.

Smith and Davis swiftly adjourned to the Tom Moody public house, where they met Elizabeth Meakin, a female acquaintance of Smith. On two occasions George left the public house to make purchases, purchases the prosecution councel at his trial were to consider very significant. George bought a gun, a charge of powder and seven or eight percussion caps. He then returned to his favourite occupation in the Tom Moody.

During the course of his conversation with the disreputable Meakin, he remarked,

"I'll do nobody any harm that does me none, but I would shoot my father if he offended me".

Returning to Ilkeston at about eight o'clock, George met Reuben Davis at the railway station, and after a brief visit to his home for some bread and cheese the pair proceeded to the Queens Head, where George resumed drinking. At some time in the evening George visited his house. On his return he told Reuben that he thought his father would commit suicide.

When the public house closed at twelve, the reluctant George returned home. Shortly afterwards a shot was heard.

Sir Frederick Pollock, the Lord Chief Baron, officiated at Smith's trial on 29 July 1861. Messrs. Boden, Huish and Cave prosecuted, while Messrs. O'Brien and Fitzjames Stephen organised Smith's defence. The evidence against George was overwhelming. Smith had stressed that his father had suicidal tendencies in order to prepare people for his sudden demise, but the forensic evidence of Dr. Norman who examined Joseph's body was conclusive.

Norman stated that in his opinion the wound could not have been self-inflicted, but must have been caused by someone standing behind the victim.

In addition, his two younger brothers both swore that on the fateful night they had heard their father quarrelling with George. They said that Joseph Smith had discovered that his passbook was missing, and had demanded to know if George had been to Nottingham. George denied this, and then they had heard a shot. A few days after the crime, Edward had found some shot and caps in the family pigsty, situated in the yard, which incidentally gives us some insight into the standards of public health prevailing in mid-nineteenth century Ilkeston.

Faced with this array of evidence, the jury found George guilty in less than two minutes.

The case caused a national furore because of the bravado exhibited by George. The national press poured forth scorn on the 'Ilkeston Parricide' for his apparent lack of remorse, reporting his quotation on being apprehended by the police.

> "Here's a heart that ne'er will fail, to swing under a gallows or under a rail".

He was executed by Calcraft on 16th August, before a huge crowd, according to the *Reporter* the biggest since that of the Heage men in 1843.

The execution itself made a deep impression on the spectators, who were perhaps becoming more sensitive to such repulsive sights. It was not one of Calcraft's finest affairs. The *Reporter* says,

> "Smith appeared to die instantly, but to those nearest the scaffold it could be seen that there was a muscular movement going on for about ten minutes before life had become quite extinct.
> The screams of women and children were awful, and the scene was a most painful one to witness.
> Stalwart men, and strong women were deeply affected and many swooned away, while others offered up audible prayers for the salvation of the unhappy wretch, whose body swung gently under a brilliant sun".

The Bloody Murder in Agard Street

Charles Wibberley, a ten year old boy, was playing in Court No. 4, Agard Street, when he saw Eliza Morrow, who lived in the court, struggling with a young man. Eliza screamed, staggered back and clutched her throat. The man ran off into Agard Street, leaving his razor by the slumped figure of his victim.

Dr. German, a surgeon who resided in Friar Gate was quickly called, but the lacerations to the throat Eliza had received caused her to expire shortly afterwards.

Ann Webster, who lodged in the same house as Eliza, and Urania Boswell, a neighbour, told Inspector Fearn of the Derby Constabulary that they had witnessed the crime, and believed Richard Thorley to be responsible.

Richard Thorley had been 'keeping company' with Eliza since the death of his wife eight months before. It seems to have been a tempestuous relationship, with Thorley blacking one of Eliza's eyes after a row in St. Helen's Street.

However, Eliza may have needed the small sums of money that Richard gave her occasionally to supplement her wages as a millhand. These wages, Ann Webster informed the court, were 7s (35p) a week full time, and 5s 4d (26½p) on short time.

Whether because of this ill-treatment of her or for other reasons, Eliza had grown tired of Richard's persistent attentions, and had started to see a soldier. Thorley had an extremely possessive nature, and became consumed with jealousy on learning this news. It appears that he met Eliza and attempted to persuade her to give up the other man. When she refused he slashed her throat with his razor.

Leaving the Court, Richard made his way to the Spa Inn on Abbey Street, where Thomas Chapman, the landlord, noticed that his hand was bandaged and covered with blood. Thorley explained that he had been involved in a fight with Irishmen in the Abbey Inn. He had two bottles of ginger beer, shook hands with the landlord, and left.

Detective Sergeant Vessey saw Thorley at 1 o'clock that night in Canal Street, and told him he was charged with the murder of Eliza. Richard replied,

"I have done it. I cannot help it now. I am sorry".

He was confined in the lock-up, and then transferred to the county gaol to await his trial.

This occurred on 24 March before Mr. Justice Williams. Mr. Yeatman, Thorley's defence counsel, tried to persuade the jury that the offence was really one of manslaughter, committed during a moment of passion. There was no 'malice aforethought' or premeditation in the crime.

Justice Williams soon disabused the jury of this notion. He pointed out the malice aforethought did not imply premeditation, but was an act committed that would deliberately result in the death of the victim.

The jury complied with this advice, and found Thorley guilty of the murder of Eliza Morrow.

More details about Thorley's life became available while he was awaiting execution. He had been born in the 'Leather Bottle Yard', Osmaston Street (now Osmaston Road) and had been employed as a striker in several foundries in Derby, the latest of which had been Messrs. Eastwood and Frost. Mr. Frost had testified at Thorley's trial that he had been a good

THE MURDERER.   **HIS VICTIM.**

RICHARD THORLEY,   ELIZA MORROW,
Executed at Derby, April 11th, 1862.   Murdered at Derby, February 13th, 1862.

Portraits of Richard Thorley and Eliza Morrow
Derby Central Library Local Studies Department

workman, and sensitive to his wife during the illness that led up to her death.

He also had aspirations as a prizefighter, and it seems that he had some success in the field. But in his last letter, an open one written to the Derby papers, he regrets that he was

> "too fond of gambling, and the alehouse, and though I am now almost ashamed to confess it, that I was one of the fraternity styling themselves the 'Derby Fancy'".

Thorley kept an appointment with William Calcraft on 11th April 1862, for what was to be Derby's last public execution. The crowd numbered ten thousand, considerably smaller than the crowd which watched the last moments of George Smith, nine months previously. The *Reporter* was gratified by this fact, but was rather disgusted to learn that one optician had been pestered by demands for telescopes and opera glasses from execution ghouls, desirous of getting a better view of the diverting spectacle.

'A Man Without Hope'
The Case of George Victor Townley

This case is one of the few Derbyshire murders to cause a national sensation. The reason it became a *cause celebre* can be attributed to the combination of three factors.

Firstly, the social status of Townley. It was rare indeed that someone from his impeccable background came to be standing in the dock indicted for the awful crime of murder.

Secondly, the case had many pathetic aspects. A tale of thwarted love with a tragic ending appealed to the sentiments of the Victorian middle classes.

Finally, and perhaps most important of all, there was heated controversy about the verdict, and the Government's handling of the case.

George Victor Townley was born in 1838, the son of a prosperous Manchester merchant. He showed signs of artistic ability almost immediately, becoming an accomplished musician by the time he was five years old. He also had a flair for languages, speaking fluent French and Latin from an early age.

However, he proved to have no ability or aptitude for the world of commerce, which was unfortunate, as this was the profession chosen for him by his father. Indeed, he was such an abject failure that his father took him from the firm to which he had been apprenticed, and employed him as a clerk in the family business.

George was a highly strung young man, with a pessimistic view of life. So pessimistic that one of the witnesses at his trial described him as a 'man without hope'. He was temperamentally incapable of sustained work, but aroused the protective instincts of his mother and sister, who doted on the unstable youth. In 1859 the Townleys were visited by the Goodwin family. Mr. and Mrs. Goodwin brought with them their nineteen year old daughter Bessie. George was attracted to her, and she reciprocated to some degree. The romance blossomed, and George and Bessie became engaged. Their relationship continued uneventfully until 1861, when the engagement was terminated. The couple continued to correspond with each other, however, and after a meeting in March 1862 they were reconciled. In the meantime, Bessie had gone to live with her grandfather, Captain Francis Goodwin, at Wigwell Grange near Wirksworth.

Townley's parents stopped with Captain Goodwin and Bessie at Wigwell in September 1862, and George's sister stayed there in January 1863. Family ties were growing, and George must have been happy with the course his romance was taking.

It must have been with some consternation, then, that he received a letter from Bessie in August of that year releasing him from the engagement.

Bessie's decision was taken at the instigation of her mother, who had decided either that Townley was of unstable character, or that he was not a good match for her daughter. The second reason seems plausible, for it later emerged that Bessie had been seeing a young clergyman who had stopped at Wigwell.

When Townley received the letter he was plunged into a state of despair. He refused anything to eat or drink, and his family were so alarmed that they asked a friend, Mr. Arrowsmith, to sit up with him. This Arrowsmith did, though he was not to find George good company, for the young man spent the night sobbing and weeping.

Wigwell Grange. Bessie Goodwin lived here with her grandfather in 1863.
photograph: Philip Taylor

When he had recovered his composure he wrote Bessie a letter asking her to meet him just once more before they parted for good.

Bessie, however was less than enthusiastic about this proposal and hastily wrote to George, forbidding him to come.

Despite this seemingly final rebuff, correspondence seems to have continued, and George eventually persuaded the reluctant Bessie to meet him. With some alacrity he caught the train, to keep an appointment with Bessie that would ultimately lead him to face a charge of murder at the County Hall in Derby.

Townley stopped at the Midland Hotel in Derby. There he was observed by a waiter pacing up and down in an agitated state. He asked the waiter where the coffee room was situated, and on receiving this information snapped at him, saying,

"I didn't want to know that".

The next day George took the train to Whatstandwell Bridge. Alighting, he first visited the Bulls Head, leaving his carpet bag with the landlady. Next, George called on the Rev. Herbert Harris, the headmaster of Wirksworth Grammar School. His intention was to extract any possible information Harris might have about his potential rival. Mr. Harris, however, said that any information he had about such a topic was confidential, and he could in no circumstances divulge it.

George decided that he would have to confront Bessie personally, so he set off for Wigwell, arriving at about 6 o'clock. Bessie was summoned, and the couple went for a walk. Half an hour later the housemaid, sent to take a message to Bessie, found them sitting on a garden seat in the plantation around the house.

George and Bessie decided to go for a longer walk, and they left the Grange grounds, turning into a lane running parallel to them, which led to Alfreton. On this path George seems to have made one last desperate attempt to get Bessie to change her mind. When this failed he cut her throat with a pocket knife.

Scene of the Wigwell murder   *photograph: Philip Taylor*

A passing farm labourer, Reuben Conway, came across Bessie staggering along the lane to the hall. George stood some distance away as if in thought, but he came back and helped Conway carry Bessie up to the Grange. George kissed her and held her in his arms, but she was beyond help, and her life ebbed away before the house could be reached.

The octagenarian Captain Goodwin, overwhelmed by the situation, invited George in for a cup of tea. The police were not so sympathetic, however, and Townley was confined in Wirksworth lock-up pending the coroner's inquest. This was held on 24th August 1863. A verdict of murder was brought in, and Townley was transported to the County Gaol to await the coming of the Assizes judge.

The trial was held on 11th December. Baron Martin presided, Mr. Boden and Mr. Bristowe represented the Crown, Mr. Macaulay, Fitzjames Stephen and Sergeant O'Brien defended Townley. The defence case rested on the grounds that Townley was insane at the time the crime was committed.

Mr. Macaulay called a host of witnesses to confirm this supposition. Many relatives testified that some of Townley's antecedents had suffered from insanity, while Bessie herself was brought in as a posthumous witness to Townley's insanity. The defence quoted a letter she had written to George's mother in March of that year. One portion of this letter said,

> "If you have any bad news I don't care about hearing it myself, so long as he is alright in body for he will not be right in mind till he gets something to do".

The witness on whom Macaulay pinned the greatest hope was the eminent psychiatric doctor Forbes Winslow. Winslow said that Townley appeared to believe that he had committed no sin, and argued that in killing Bessie he was repossessing himself of property that had been stolen. He also appeared to think that there was a conspiracy against him.

Mr. Gisbourne, the surgeon to the County Gaol, stated that while he thought that Townley knew that what he had done was wrong, nevertheless,

> "I consider him to be of unsound mind".

Despite this impressive evidence, Baron Martin was no more prepared to accept that great stress, or emotional illness, constituted sufficient grounds for evasion of criminal responsibilities than any other trial judge of that period. The notion that temporary insanity was possible was not generally held to be acceptable.

The jury found Townley guilty, and Baron Martin passed sentence of death. He was visibly moved, and broke down several times before he could finish. The *Reporter* notes that,

> "Many parties in court sobbed audibly".

A campaign was immediately launched to secure a commutation of Townley's sentence. A petition in Manchester gained sixteen thousand signatures, while nine of the jurymen wrote to the Home Secretary asking for a respite on the grounds that the action was unpremeditated. Derby's petition included over three hundred signatures from the worthy inhabitants of the area round Wigwell itself.

The Home Secretary, Sir George Grey, was more impressed by a letter from Baron Martin, pointing out that the defence had been one of insanity, and suggesting that further investigations might be appropriate. On receipt of this information, Sir George appointed three Lunacy Commissioners to examine Townley.

Meanwhile, Townley's defence solicitors had discovered a little used act which allowed medical men and magistrates to request examination of prisoners where mental illness was suspected as a cause of criminal behaviour.

Five men including Thomas Roe, the Mayor, and Dr. Harwood, the surgeon to the Poor Law Union, went to see Townley themselves. Afterwards they declared that they believed Townley to be insane.

The Lunacy Commissioners had reported to Sir George Grey, in the meantime, that though Townley was capable of knowing what he had done was wrong, he was 'not of sound mind'. Grey acted on this information, and Townley was sent to Bethlem Hospital.

The decision caused a tremendous outcry. The working classes saw the Townley reprieve as a prime example of class discrimination. At the same time as George was reprieved Samuel Wright, a brickmaker, was executed for the murder of his wife during a domestic dispute. The Wright case had none of the interesting features of the Townley affair.

Wright was arraigned for the murder, attended the coroner's inquest, took his trial and was executed all in the space of one short week.

He had pleaded guilty, and had no defence counsel. The crowds at his execution booed and jeered the hangman, and shouted, "Where's Townley?". A handbill was distributed amongst the crowd. It said,

> "Shall Wright be hung? If so then there is one law for the rich, and another for the poor".

In Derby, controversy still raged. Some of the Derby bench, who disapproved of the reprieve, blamed Roe and his delegation for the decision.

They wrote to the Home Secretary complaining that they had not been consulted. They complained that the spirit of the act had been violated, for in this case the initiative had not received the blessing of the entire Derbyshire bench, but had come only from Townley's defence counsel. They thought that the case had established an unfortunate precedent, giving rise to the belief that there was one law for the rich, and another for the poor.

Sir George retorted that he had appointed the Lunacy Commissioners on the advice of Baron Martin, and had not been influenced by the urgings of the Derby party.

The Derbyshire row over Townley's reprieve was mirrored at a national level. The correspondence columns of *The Times*, *Daily Telegraph* and *Spectator* were filled with letters about the case, and floods of books and pamphlets were produced on the subject. A pamphlet by C. Robertson and H. Maudslay called 'Insanity and Crime' for example, which attacked the decision to reprieve Townley on the grounds that his insanity had not been satisfactorily proved, brought forth an immediate rejoinder from Richard

Portraits of George Townley and Bessie Goodwin
Derby Central Library Local Studies Department

Hardwicke. His pamphlet, 'A Voice from Derby to Bedlam', pointed out that most of the people who examined Townley believed that he was mentally ill.

However, the harsh regime of a nineteenth century prison was too much for the unstable man. In February 1865 George Victor Townley committed suicide by jumping over the staircase at Pentonville Prison.

James Potter: Bound for Broadmoor

James Potter lived with his wife at 59 Traffic Street, Derby, in a state of marital warfare.

Potter had been employed as a sheriff's bailiff, but had lost this position due to his strange behaviour several months before.

Apparently, James could not be trusted to go to the right houses, and often forgot the purpose for which he had been sent.

The Potters had frequent rows and fights when Potter came home drunk from the alehouse. The unhappy matrimonial home was subjected to further stress when the Potters, by now struggling to make ends meet, took in a lodger called John Stone. Potter became convinced that Stone and his wife were guilty of improper behaviour.

On 22nd December 1864, Potter threatened his wife to such an extent that she ran from the house and took refuge in an entry. She was later persuaded to return by her daughter. It was a fateful decision.

That night her husband ran her through with a sword-stick.

He was fortunate enough to be defended by James Fitzjames Stephen at his trial on 13th March 1865.

Stephen pleaded that insanity lay at the root of the crime. His summing up, lasted one hour and thirty-five minutes and was, according to the *Mercury,*

> "One of the most eloquent, and impressive addresses ever made in a court of justice".

The speech, though, made little difference to the outcome of the trial, for Potter was sentenced to death.

The Home Secreatry commuted the death sentence, however, after hearing the medical evidence presented at the trial, and sent Potter to Broadmoor Lunatic Asylum.

This decision, coming on the heels of the Townley verdict in which the question of sanity had also been at issue, aroused a clamour in the local press. Mr. Gisborne, the prison surgeon, wrote to say that he had examined Potter, and thought him criminally responsible.

But when a resident of Derby wrote to the superintendent physician of Broadmoor, inquiring as to Potter's condition, he was told rather unfeelingly,

> "In his mental state there is very little change. If anything he requires now less watching than on admission. His condition is that of muttering, incoherent imbecility. He is not likely to recover from this condition".

James Potter died in Broadmoor several years later.

Death in the Deep Rake

This crime took place at a remote farmhouse, Bleaklow Farm, near Great Longstone.

Richard Sellors and his son Roger, lead miners living at Stoney Middleton, were to observe the final scenes in this tragedy. Returning from work they saw a woman running towards them from the farm, which lay on high ground. She was being hotly pursued by a man. Between them and the couple lay a dam situated in the Deep Rake, a steep cutting made by lead miners. This dam shelved sharply from its rim to the edge of the water.

The woman cried out to the Sellors that she was being murdered. As the Sellors reached the top of the bank leading to the water they saw the man throw the woman down, and proceed to kick and ill-treat her. Then they saw the woman slide into the water.

The woman was Harriet Wager, and the man ill-treating her was her husband of only six weeks, Edward Wager, who farmed at Bleaklow. By the time he had finished beating her Wager had irrevocably terminated his marriage for poor Harriet never emerged from the waters alive.

Harriet Wager was about forty at the time of her death. She had two sons from a previous marriage, the elder of whom was a soldier, and a bone of contention between her and her husband. The younger, Benjamin Oliver, was twelve and lived with the Wagers at Bleaklow.

Harriet was not a raving beauty. The medical evidence at the trial of Dr. Wrench, a surgeon from Baslow, reveals that she was very stout, and from the condition of her liver a heavy drinker. She was also totally bald, which she successfully disguised by wearing a wig.

Despite her rather unprepossessing appearance, the unfortunate Harriet formed a liason with Wager, then aged thirty-six. The relationship had continued for three years before the marriage.

Wager appears to have had the same predilection for drink as his wife, for on the day of her murder, Christmas Eve 1866, he had been drinking heavily in the Newburgh Arms at Hassop. He had also been drinking the night before, which had resulted in Harriet seeking shelter in the house of the Hancock family. Harriet knew from bitter experience that Edward could be very violent when in his cups.

Mrs. Hancock had been an old friend of hers, and Harriet asked her if her daughter Alice would accompany her back to Bleaklow. She obviously believed that her husband would not abuse or assault her in the presence of company. She was soon to realise that she was labouring under a misapprehension.

When she arrived at Bleaklow, Edward swore at her, demanded to know where she had been, and then pushed her out of the house, saying,

"Go away where you've been, you shall not stay here".

Wager was obviously drunk and in a nasty mood, so after

tea Mrs. Wager crept out of the house and hid under a shed in the farmyard. Alice Hancock came out to find her, and because the weather was bitterly cold told her to go back to the house and collect her cloak.

Edward Wager had other ideas, and drove his cattle round to block the gate so that Harriet and Alice could not escape. When Alice tried to climb over the wall he pulled her back, saying,

> "Come back, you'll not go from here tonight".

Harriet intervened on Alice's behalf, and Wager chased her across the fields and over two stone walls, until he caught up with her near the Deep Rake. It was there that the Sellors were to witness the last moments of Mrs. Wager's life.

William Goddard, a miner, following in the footsteps of the Sellors found the body floating in the dam, and fetched Inspector Cruitt from Stoney Middleton. They took the body out of the water and carried it back to the farmhouse, where Mr. Cruitt interrogated Wager. Wager appeared unconcerned about the death, saying only,

> "Ah, thou poor ignorant bugger, thou has drowned thyself at last".

Wager stuck to this story at the police station. According to him, Harriet had tried to drown herself, and he had followed to try and prevent her.

The evidence of Dr. Wrench contradicted this version of events. He said that Harriet had a broken nose, lacerated mouth, and a ruptured liver, injuries consistent with those likely to have been administered by a heavy boot. Wrench concluded that the injuries to the liver would probably have resulted in Harriet's death eventually, but that the actual cause of death was drowning.

The trial took place in March 1867. Mr. Maule led for the Crown. Mr. Fitzjames Stephen appeared for the defence. Mr. Stephen encouraged the jury to accept that the drowning was accidental, the woman drowning herself to escape the brutality of her husband.

But his lordship, Sir Robert Lush, intervened and said that

Bleaklow Farm, near Great Longstone   *photograph: Philip Taylor*

manslaughter was not an acceptable verdict, and that the death was either murder or suicide. He told the jury that if Wager had deliberately pushed Harriet in the water it was obviously murder, but the case would still be one of murder if they thought Mrs. Wager had jumped into the water preferring one death to another.

The jury found Wager guilty of murder, but recommended him to mercy on the grounds that he did not know what he was doing at the time.

Wager was subsequently reprieved, and ordered to serve penal servitude for life.

'It Looks Like Hell-fire'

Samuel Wallis was a shoemaker who lived in Chesterfield with his wife and two young children.

Mrs. Wallis worked as a dressmaker to supplement the family income and the Wallises, unlike many of the Victorian working classes, seem to have been free of the pervading fear of poverty.

Their potential bliss was blighted by one major problem,

that of Samuel's mental state. He had conceived the notion that he was suffering from an incurable disease. No amount of reassurance could dissuade him from this notion, and it preyed upon his mind to such an extent that he became heavily depressed, and incapable of work.

On the night of 8th November 1871, Samuel's already shaken grip on reality snapped completely. He slashed his wife's throat with a knife, showering his eldest son, seven year old George, with blood in the process.

Once again the motivation for the crime was alleged to be insanity. Even the prosecution were prepared to admit that Wallis was unstable.

Police Constable Walsh, who had taken Samuel from Chesterfield by train to the County Gaol, remembered that he was extremely agitated. Pointing to the setting sun Wallis had said excitably,

"Look, it looks like Hell-fire".

The jury found Wallis guilty of wilful murder, but recommended him to mercy, on account of the weakness of his mind.

As a result, his sentence was commuted, and he was ordered to be confined at Broadmoor.

'Ben Hudson's Heart I Mean To Turn'

George Goaling, a shoemaker, was walking along the road from Middle to West Handley when to his horror he discovered the body of a woman. Running back along the road Goaling observed Charles Evans standing in his cottage garden, which adjoined the lane.

He persuaded Evans to accompany him, and the pair returned to the body to await the arrival of the local constable. The latter retrieved a hedge stake that lay by the side of the body, which he rightfully took to be the murder weapon, and the three men carried the corpse to the Devonshire Arms. In the woman's pockets were found a note and a box of pins.

The Devonshire Arms, Middle Handley *photograph: Philip Taylor*

The dead woman was Eliza Hudson, the estranged wife of Benjamin Hudson, a twenty-eight year old collier. He promptly became the suspect for the crime.

Eliza was a woman with a notorious reputation, for she had conceived a child by James Hibbert, and another by a man named Holmes before she married Benjamin. Nevertheless the twenty-one year old Benjamin seems to have conceived a liking for his elder cousin. The relationship ripened into intimacy, and Eliza was delivered of another illegitimate child before the couple were married. They moved first into a cottage at Handley, and later to one in Lightwood, a nearby hamlet.

The marriage, however, was not a success, and Benjamin Hudson soon found an outlet for his frustrations by frequently assaulting his wife.

Eliza was not entirely blameless for this state of affairs, for it seems she was still seeing Hibbert, and Benjamin's growing fears about her faithfulness may not have been altogether groundless. Hudson was bound over to keep the peace several times after ill-treating Eliza and on one occasion was even sent to gaol.

Eventually Eliza could take this no longer, and after a particularly brutal assault she finally left him and went to stay with her father.

Eliza was too scared to return to her husband, and she sought a legal separation from him. This was granted shortly afterwards, Benjamin agreeing to pay five shillings a week maintenance to Eliza and the children. He sold the family furniture and went to stay with one of his numerous West Handley relatives.

Benjamin was bitter, resentful and tormented by the thought of his wife's relationship with Hibbert. He took to following Eliza about and threatening her.

On the evening of 23rd April, Benjamin was at the house of John Morton, a fellow collier. He told Morton that his wife was keeping company with other men, and that the man she had lived with before had offered him a sovereign for her. Morton was to confirm that there was something going on between Hibbert and Eliza. At the trial he testified that Hibbert had told him that he was going to Eliza's house to fetch her. Benjamin told John that if he was to give him a gun he would shoot her and the old ————— too.

On the following day, Eliza was returning home after washing some clothes for Mrs. Hardwick at Lightwood, an old neighbour of the Hudsons.

Hudson followed her and, according to his own account, they met on Bowman Lane, which ran between Middle and West Handley. The couple had a blistering row which ended when Benjamin tore a stake out of the hedge and beat Eliza to death with it.

He then called on one of his relatives, a man called Cope. He told Cope and John Hudson, yet another of his relatives, that he had killed his wife and that he was going to hang himself. He was discovered at the house by P.C. Hookin and Charles Evans, and admitted responsibility.

At the trial on 15th July, which was conducted by Mr. Justice Honyman, Hudson's defence counsel, Mr. Waddy, argued that the crime was one of manslaughter. He pointed out that the crime was unpremeditated. Hudson had not come with a weapon prepared to commit the murder, but had

The footpath leading from Middle to West Handley where Eliza Hudson was murdered
photograph: Philip Taylor

needed to pull up a nearby stake. He also submitted that Hudson had received great provocation by reason of his wife's behaviour.

Mr. Buszard, who led for the Crown, stressed to the jury that the law would only accept provocation as a mitigating factor if it was in circumstances where the deceased had struck the first blow in a quarrel. In this instance there was no evidence to suggest that this was the case.

The jury took nearly two hours to reach a decision. They found Hudson guilty of murder, but recommended him to mercy on the grounds of the unhappy life he had led. The *Mercury* records that,

> "The Judge was affected to tears, and frequently sobbed as he was passing sentence".

The Reverend Ollivier, chaplain to the High Sheriff, was so impressed by Hudson's penitence as he awaited death that he resolved to visit the Home Secretary personally to plead for a reprieve. The Secretary, Henry Bruce, received him on 1st August, but stressed that he would only listen to a plea for clemency if it were put in writing. As the execution was fixed for 4th August, the following Monday, this gave Ollivier very little time to drum up support for a reprieve. The petition which was sent to London had very few signatures as a consequence, and the Home Secretary informed Ollivier that there was insufficient reason to commute the sentence.

The town of Derby buzzed with excitement at the news. One of the few disappointed people was a certain Mrs. German, of Uttoxeter Road, She requested to see Benjamin because,

> "It was borne in her by the spirit that she should see him, as she could do him good and had the power to unlock men's hearts".

Whatever the spirit might have wanted, the Governor of the prison declined to accept her generous invitation, and Benjamin was deprived of his unusual visitor.

Benjamin Hudson was executed by William Marwood, the famous, or should it be infamous Victorian executioner. Marwood was just beginning his illustrious career, which was to see him succeed William Calcraft, the official public executioner, the following year, and this was only his second execution.

This was the first private execution in Derby, as the Execution Within Prisons Act of 1868 had been passed since the last execution, that of Richard Thorley in 1862. Under the provisions of the new Act, attendance was restricted to the Governor of the prison, the Sheriff's officers, warders and representatives of the press.

Notwithstanding this, several hundred people congregated outside the prison to hear the bell toll, and a black flag hoisted on 4th August.

Hudson was executed holding a bouquet of flowers given to him by his aunt.

One of the more pathetic aspects of the case was the existence of the note and box of pins found on Eliza's body. She had apparently still retained some residue of affection for Benjamin despite his ill-treatment of her, for the note, which was in the form of a rhyme, stated,

> "It is not these pins I mean to burn
> But Ben Hudson's heart I mean to turn,
> May he neither eat, speak, drink nor comfort find,
> Till he comes to me and speaks his mind".

The tone of this note suggests that it was some kind of charm. Was it obtained from some village wiseman or conjuror? We shall never know. But in this case the charm seems to have lacked potency, with disastrous consequences for all concerned.

The Murder of a Ninety Nine Year Old Man

Rose Brown, aged fifty-seven, lived with her ninety-nine year old husband in Bag Lane (now East Street) in Derby.

Looking after the old man, who was crippled, was a trial for Rose. There were frequent quarrels, probably about money, for poor William Brown's only occupation appears to have been selling shoelaces in Derby Market place. The row they had on 12th June 1875, appears to have been more bitter than any preceding, however, for it ended with Rose clubbing her aged husband over the head with a poker, causing him injuries from which he eventually expired.

The jury found Rose guilty of murder, but recommended her to mercy on account of her age. The Home Secretary took this plea into account and her sentence was commuted to one of penal servitude for life.

Drink and the Devil

This case became a national *cause celebre* for three reasons.

Firstly, the social status of the accused. It was very rare that anyone from Mainwaring's background (he was described in his indictment as a gentleman) had to stand trial for murder.

Secondly, drink was a major factor in the commission of the crime, which was committed at the height of the temperance campaign. The Victorian public were shocked by the publication of the figures for the consumption of drink in the mid-1870s, which was the highest ever recorded. 1875 saw the peak figures for the consumption of spirits, and the following year the consumption of beer equivalent to 34.4 gallons per year for each individual in the country.

Contemporaries were worried that Britain was going to degenerate into a nation of alcoholics and wastrels. There was an instant backlash. Temperance societies experienced a rapid growth, and they attempted to exert pressure on the government to pass legislation severely limiting the number of licences granted to publicans. The links between drink and crime were recognised, and they provided ammunition for those seeking to attack the drinking of alcohol.

A letter to the *Leicester Daily Post* in 1877, about a murder in that city, sums up the attitude felt by many in the Derby area. Under the heading 'Licensed Murder', the writer says,

> *"The law allows drink to be sold, and then because some poor fellows who have stupified themselves with it fall out and fight, one is killed and the others we hang for it".*

The sight of a young gentleman like Mainwaring reduced to such circumstances seemed to underline the point that drink could only lead to disgrace and humiliation. Local temperance societies were able to make great capital out of the occurrence.

The third factor was to be the controversial way in which the jury in the Mainwaring case arrived at their verdict.

Gerald Mainwaring was a wealthy playboy, the son of the Reverend Edward Mainwaring, a Staffordshire magistrate who lived at Whitmore Hall, on the Derbyshire-Staffs border.

At the time of his condemnation this ne'er-do-well was embarking on a drinking spree in Derby preparatory to being packed off by his outraged parents to Manitoba, to start a new life as a farmer. Gerald's farewell fling in Derby started on 10th July 1879, when he entered the shop of Euphemia Dobson in the Market Place, and purchased a revolver and five hundred cartridges. Next he proceeded to the Royal Hotel in Victoria Street for liquid refreshment, a habit to which he was to have frequent recourse during his short but eventful stay in Derby.

By now well fuelled Gerald decided to seek out some feminine company, so he proceeded to a brothel at 20 Bradshaw Street, administered by a Mrs. Gilbert. He asked if he could avail himself of the facilities, and was introduced to Miss Annie Green. It was an introduction he was to bitterly regret before two days had elapsed.

Having spent the night with Annie he hired a cab and, with her in tow, he departed to the Royal Hotel, where he spent the rest of the day drinking.

He returned to Bradshaw Street that night, and repeating the pattern of the previous day he decamped to the Royal with Annie for a late breakfast, which seems to have had a strong alcoholic base. According to a waitress, Fanny Davis, she served the couple three pints of claret and a quart bottle of brandy.

By now thoroughly inebriated the dissolute pair visited Bradshaw Street, where Mainwaring asked Mrs. Gilbert if he could 'borrow' Annie for two or three days. Mrs. Gilbert refused, as she could see Annie was much the worse for wear, and said that she ought to go and lie down.

Gerald flew into a rage, and taking out his revolver started to load it in front of Mrs. Gilbert. He was so incensed at being thwarted that he dropped three cartridges on the floor. These were later retrieved by the police and formed part of the evidence at the trial. Pointing the gun at Mrs. Gilbert, Mainwaring said,

"Now will you let her go?"

The terrified madam said,

"Yes, take her for God's sake and go".

Gerald and Annie thereupon jumped into their trap and made off erratically, in the direction of the city centre.

Here their trap was observed by Constable Clamp, careering down Victoria Street. He persued it down Friar Gate, where it was to be seen going round in circles under the railway bridge.

By now Clamp had been joined in the pursuit by two colleagues, Constables' Slaney and Moss. The intrepid trio caught up with the trap in the yard of the 'Travellers Rest' in

The Travellers Rest, Ashbourne Road, Derby. Gerald Mainwaring was arrested by the police in the yard of the inn   *photograph: Philip Taylor*

Ashbourne Road, where Mainwaring greeted them with the words

> "My father is a magistrate in Staffordshire. Come and have something to drink and say no more about it".

The policeman were not swayed by this generosity, and Mainwaring and his companion were brought back to the lock-up, to be charged with the offence of being drunk in charge of a horse and trap.

It was here that the tragedy occurred. Inspector Spibey was preparing to take a statement from them when Annie Green started to scream that she would not be locked up. She struck Constable Clamp across the face. Constable Moss took firm hold of her arms, whereupon Mainwaring drew his revolver and shot Moss through the chest. P.C. Price put his head down and rushed Gerald, who fired again, putting a bullet through Price's helmet. A third bullet hit Price in the left arm. Eventually after a desperate struggle in which another shot rang out, Inspector Spibey wrestled the gun from Mainwaring's hand, and he was overpowered.

Moss died the following day at the Derbyshire Infirmary, and Colonel Delacombe, the Chief Constable, had the responsibility of telling Mainwaring that he was to stand trial for the murder of Moss.

The trial duly took place on 7th August. Mr. Justice Lindley presiding. Mr. Lawrence Q.C. led for the Crown, while Mainwaring had the services of the Solicitor General, Sir Hardinge Gifford, who was retained at a cost of 400 guineas.

Gifford argued that the crime was committed under circumstances that reduced the offence from murder to manslaughter. In this case drink, Gifford believed, had produced such an effect on Mainwaring that he was not responsible for his actions.

But Justice Lindley ruled that,

> "It must not be understood that because a man was drunk he was not possessed of any will at all. Some years ago there was a discussion on the subject by some judges, and they came to the conclusion that drunkenness did not in any way excuse murder, or in any way justify a jury in reducing a case of murder to one of manslaughter".

The jury retired at one o'clock, and returned at twenty past four to bring in a verdict of guilty, but with a strong recommendation to mercy.

A petition was got up to try to secure a reprieve, and it was signed by 5,720 people. But while this was proceeding, a bitter controversy about the way in which the jury had reached its verdict was to eclipse the formal attempts to secure commutation of the death penalty.

A reporter from the *Times* had interviewed Mr. Astle, the foreman of the jury, and an astonishing fact apparently emerged. Astle was quoted as saying that the jury had been unable to reach a verdict, and had split 6-6 on the decision. The jury had then balloted for a decision. The agreement was that the drawer of the blank card should decide the verdict.

This account reached the ears of the Home Secretary, Richard Cross, who was then forced to answer a number of awkward questions about the decision by outraged M.P.s. Cross threatened to prosecute the jury if the story was found to be true, and launched an immediate inquiry. Two days later he was able to read to the House a letter he had received from Mr. Astle, which read,

> Sir,
>
> In reply to your inquiry respecting the mode in which the jury in the Gerald Mainwaring case came to reach their decision. I beg to state that after the jury had retired it was ascertained that they were equally divided as to their verdict, six being for manslaughter, and six for wilful murder, with a strong recommendation to mercy.
>
> We had not then selected a chairman, and I as foreman declined to act as such. A chairman was balloted for, and it was agreed that the vote of the majority should carry the verdict and if it were again equally divided, the chairman was to have the casting vote.
>
> There was no casting vote for the verdict, but only balloting for the chairman, and I wish this to be made public to the fullest extent so as to contradict many untrue reports which have been circulated".

Mr. Cross, however, did not see Mr. Astle's fine distinctions in this matter, and in consequence of these irregularities, he cancelled the death sentence, and substituted one of penal servitude for life.

The national press reported the case in detail, and the jury came in for a great deal of criticism. The *Spectator*, for example, thought that the Derby jury should have been sued.

But this was not to be the end of the controversy.

Mr. Kent of Duffield, the man who had been elected Chairman of the jury, wrote a letter to the *Derby Mercury* contradicting Mr. Astle's account. Mr. Kent stated that, he had not been responsible for a casting vote.

> "Indeed before leaving the room, the foreman several times asked if all were agreed, and no objection was made by anyone of the jurors to the verdict, as it was returned".

Another juror, Mr. Tempest, the assistant overseer, confirmed this account.

But other jurors wrote to the *Reporter* disputing Mr. Kent's version, and supporting Mr. Astle's original version sent to Mr. Cross. In the end four jurors supported Mr. Astle's version, and two Mr. Kent's.

As the *Reporter* said at the time,

> "Surely a more remarkable picture of contradiction was never seen".

It concluded,

> "It would appear that the hopes of an adjustment of the curious difficulty must now be abandoned".

Thus ended the Mainwaring case, though ripples from the case were to continue for a few weeks more.

The Temperance movement was to make capital out of the affair. On the Sunday after Mainwaring's conviction a sermon was preached against the evils of drink in St. Luke's Church in Derby. In Parliament Sir Wilfred Lawson, a leading temperance crusader, inquired of Mr. Cross what action would be taken against the licensee of the Royal Hotel, a man many temperance advocates saw as the real villain in the case. Mr. Cross was able to placate Sir Wilfred by announcing that the Chief Constable of Derby was to take the unfortunate licensee, Mr. Charles Taylor, to court.

However, Sir Wilfred would have been less pleased if he had learnt that Mr. Taylor was merely fined £3 and given a stern lecture on the wickedness of drink.

The Spectre of Death

Thomas Spooner Litherland was to take his trial at the same Assizes as Mainwaring. His case did not lead to any national publicity, yet the two cases were to become linked in the public mind, because of the contrast in the way the two men were treated.

Litherland was a bricklayer, who lived with his wife Sarah

and five children at 20 Eldon Buildings, Winshill, near Burton-on-Trent.

There was no history of sustained dometic violence between Litherland and his wife, but several witnesses at his trial were to testify to Litherland's odd behaviour. He had, apparently, threatened to kill his wife three months previously, and had contemplated suicide on several occasions. Samuel had also told his sister that he had encountered a spectre with a knife, standing by the pump in the yard. He had refused to accept that this was an illusion.

On 21st June 1879, Litherland accompanied by several friends paid a visit to the Anglesey Arms. He returned at tea-time and sent his children out to play. Then he cut his wife's throat with a knife. When the police arrived, Thomas commented,

> "I cannot think what made me do it. We have always been so comfortable".

He was sentenced to death, and the decision caused an outcry.

Many observers were quick to draw comparisons between the treatment accorded Litherland, a poor bricklayer, and the wealthy Mainwaring. It was generally agreed that it would be outrageous if Litherland were to hang, while Mainwaring escaped the noose.

They need not have worried, however. The magistrate who had originally remanded Litherland petitioned Mr. Cross for a reprieve, on the grounds of insanity. Two medical examiners were despatched to examine Litherland, as a consequence.

They reported that Thomas was insane. Cross acted swiftly, and the unfortunate bricklayer was removed to Broadmoor. This decision, says the *Mercury*, was 'hailed with decided approval'.

The Shocking Outrage in Court Number One

Elizabeth Wilkinson was worried. She and her younger sister Ellen had been selling cardboard comb boxes in the vicinity of Bridge Street. In order to speed up their task the girls had separated, Elizabeth directing her sister to Court No. 1 off Green Street, also known as Tanyard Court. Elizabeth soon disposed of her wares, and patiently awaited the arrival of her nine year old sister.

Time passed, but Ellen failed to put in an appearance. Elizabeth went home thinking that Ellen must have finished her task first and returned home without informing her. But Ellen was not there.

By now thoroughly alarmed, Elizabeth retraced her steps to Court No. 1 and searched frantically for her sister.

At last, in house no. 13, she found her. Ellen Wilkinson lay at the foot of a flight of stairs. Her throat had been cut. By her hand lay the knife with which the injuries had been inflicted, a pill-box containing a few grain of oats, and a halfpenny. On a table stood the little comb box she had been attempting to sell.

The house was occupied by a Mrs. Wakefield and her two sons. Before the family could be investigated, however, one of the sons, John Wakefield, walked into the police station and confessed to the crime. Wakefield told Inspector Barnes that he had committed a murder, and would like to see the Chief Constable. Barnes was not inclined to give any credence to this story at first, thinking that Wakefield was a crank. But Wakefield persisted, so Barnes fetched Colonel Delacombe.

Delacombe summoned Inspector Spibey and Sergeant Oxter, and they proceeded to Wakefield's house to check out his story. They soon realised that Wakefield was in earnest, and he was indicted for the murder of Ellen Wilkinson.

Information about Wakefield's character which emerged after the trial reveal him to have been very strange indeed. Wakefield was twenty-eight years old at the time, and the *Mercury* reports that he had 'a head very large in proportion to his body'. He seems to have had a temperamental antipathy to work and was incapable of holding down a job for long. He had formerly been employed by Messrs. Latham and Oliver, but had been out of work for some time.

This state of affairs seems to have suited the morbid John who much preferred to spend his time in looking after the domestic arrangements of the Wakefield household. The *Reporter* notes disparagingly that he indulged in such unmanly occupations as washing clothes and doing the family shopping.

His mother also testified that John was given to violent outbursts of temper, and that she had feared that he would commit suicide.

Wakefield appeared at the County Hall on 28th July to answer a charge of wilful murder. Mr. Stanger took on the task of defending Wakefield at only a few hours notice. He attempted to convince the jury that the murder had been committed in a moment of uncontrollable passion. Mr. Wright Baker, the surgeon to the County Gaol, agreed that such an act would be done in this way. But the prosecution pointed out that no evidence had been offered which suggested that the prisoner was suffering from mental disease, and there was no evidence that the prisoner was subject to impulses of this kind.

The jury decided that Wakefield was guilty, and Baron Huddleston sentenced him to death.

He told Wakefield that he could hold out little hope of a reprieve. The Derbyshire public, too, overwhelmingly believed that Wakefield should hang for such a shocking murder. However, some attempt was made to secure mitigation of the sentence. A petition arguing that Wakefield might be insane was signed by many of Derby's prominent citizens, probably anxious to avoid the stigma of a hanging in the town.

Sir William Harcourt, the Home Secretary, investigated the case but could see little reason for commuting the death sentence.

Wakefield was hanged by William Marwood on 16th August 1880. According to the *Mercury*, as the priest intoned the phrase 'man that is born of woman hath but a short time to live' the drop was released, and Wakefield was launched into eternity.

'You will Not See Me Alive Again'

This case highlights the social stigma of illegitimacy in Victorian Britain, and illustrates all too vividly the desperate situation in which unmarried women could find themselves when they become pregnant.

Mary Wright was arraigned for the murder of her illegitimate child at the Summer Assizes in 1880. Mary had drowned the child in a pond on Bonsall Moor, after a traumatic interview with her father.

She had become emotionally entangled with a farm servant employed by her father, with the result that she became pregnant once more. When she broached the subject with Mr. Henry Abbott he decided that he was not prepared to take his parental responsibilities very seriously, and decamped forthwith.

Mary was desperate, but when she summoned up the courage to tell her father he said angrily,

"If you do these things you must leave the house".

Mary wandered out onto the moor at night, and tried to drown herself and the child.

There was a great deal of sympathy for Mary, and though the jury found her guilty of murder, the judge did not assume the black cap, as he thought it unlikely that the sentence would be carried out.

Sir William Harcourt later commuted the sentence to one of life imprisonment.

Albert Robinson
The Hadfield Killer

Albert Robinson was only twenty when he married Jane Eliza, the thirty year old widow of James Sidebottom. Jane had once been a respectable lady. According to the *Reporter*, she had been a prominent scholar in the Sunday School, and an active participant in the drama society of Hadfield.

The death of her husband, who was a mason by trade, left Jane with the responsibilty of bringing up two young children, Frank aged seven at the time the tragedy occurred, and William aged three.

Like many other Victorian women in her predicament, Jane was soon in desperate financial straits. It was during this period that her reputation began to suffer. She found it a struggle to keep up the toll-bar at Hirstclough that she had previously managed with her husband's help. She soon took to frequenting the local public houses, where she encountered Albert Robinson. Robinson was a dissolute youth, fond of drinking and wenching, who had already fathered an illegitimate child on a girl named Schofield at Tintwhistle.

He became Jane's steady boyfriend, and in the early months of 1880 they were married, much to the surprise of Jane's friends, who wondered why she had decided to become involved with such a ne'er-do-well. But, as Jane herself remarked, what else was she to do? Her friends and relations had all disowned her, and she had two young children to think of.

The marriage was doomed from the start. Albert had no intention of letting his new responsibilities interfere with the continuation of his old lifestyle. Albert continued drinking and carousing long after the family had moved into Station Street, Hadfield.

On the day of the murder, 4th October 1880, Robinson and his wife had a row about a box which contained sixteen shillings (80p) saved by Jane for emergencies. Later it transpired that Robinson had needed the money for the maintenance of his illegitimate child.

Albert came home at a quarter past four to find his wife the worse for wear for drink. Ellen Campbell, who lodged with the Robinson's was to witness the quarrel that led to Jane's death. Robinson accused his wife of spreading tales about him to the neighbours, and of getting money for drink from other men, claims which Jane totally denied. Albert lost his temper and produced a penknife, threatening to stab her.

Ellen ran out of the house to get help, and while she was gone Albert slashed his wife's throat. This murder was observed by Jane's eldest son.

Abraham Hearnshaw saw Albert run out of the house, and went to fetch Inspector Charlton. Charlton's first hunch was to visit Robinson's mother, who resided at the Bulls Head in Mottram, but Albert was not on the premises. However, on a subsequent nocturnal call to this address in the early morning, Charlton discovered Albert Robinson lying across the sofa in the living room. His throat had been cut.

Dr. Binns was called and treated the gash, which was three inches long. Robinson recovered, however, and he was indicted for the murder of his wife.

The trial took place on 10th February 1881. Mr. Justice Denman officiated, and Robinson was defended by Mr. Etherington Smith.

Etherington Smith made a forlorn attempt to persuade the jury that Robinson was mentally ill, instancing his attempt at suicide as evidence of his instability. But none of the witnesses could be persuaded to say that Robinson was insane, and Dr. Wright Baker said that Robinson "spoke like any other man".

The jury found Robinson guilty of his wife's murder, and his execution was fixed for 28th February.

Because the crime occurred in a remote part of Derbyshire it created little interest amongst the townspeople of Derby. There was thus a reluctance to get up a petition on Robinson's behalf. Eventually, however, Lord Howard of Glossop made a belated attempt to achieve clemency for Robinson, on account of his youth, Robinson not having yet reached the age of majority. It received few signatures, but the Home Secretary sent a team of medical men to examine Robinson. They reported that Robinson had no mental abnormalities, so the Home Secretary saw no reason to intervene.

Robinson was executed by William Marwood. A crowd of five hundred gathered outside the prison at the time of the execution, but only the representative of the *Mercury* was allowed to observe the execution. He reported that Robinson's death was instantaneous.

The Horrible Discovery in Hooles Plantation

On a bright summer day in August, 1881, little Eleanor Windle was playing with her friends at Brimington. After a while, the children decided to go blackberrying at Tinkersick, which lay n the direction of Chesterfield. While they were absorbed in this occupation Alfred Gough, a hawker, appeared on the scene.

Gough was a great favourite with the children of the area, for apart from plying his trade as a rag and bone man he sold small toys, such as parasols and windmills, from his hand cart. Eleanor had set her heart on a toy parasol and, recollecting that her mother was keeping a halfpenny for her, she followed Gough back towards Brimington, leaving her playmates to their task. They were never to see her again.

John Insley, a carrier, saw the incongrous pair at the bottom of Johnson's Lane. Miss Harriet Johnson, who lived in Oak House which overlooked the lane, thought there was something suspicious in this relationship. She left her house to investigate. What she saw horrified her.

Gough was in the act of exposing himself to the little girl. Harriet got a broom handle and went after them. But she was unable to catch them, and went home.

John Cook, a labourer who worked on the highway, came across Gough's handcart standing at the bottom of the lane, still complete with its load of rags. Cook waited to see if someone would turn up to claim their property, but when the owner failed to put in an appearance he went off to pick mushrooms.

When he returned the handcart had vanished. At about eleven thirty Sarah Cantrill saw the handcart being wheeled by Gough. She noticed that the cart contained something large, over which rags had been thrown.

Gough stopped at the tollhouse kept by a man rejoicing in the name of Charles Hastings Abney Brown, for a glass of ginger beer. While he was there, the distraught father of Eleanor Windle arrived. Mr. Windle asked Gough some searching questions about the girl, but only received evasive answers. Gough said,

> "Are you the father of the child?"

Windle replied,

> "I am".

Gough said,

> "I am sorry, it is a bad job".

Windle left and walked to the Three Horse Shoes in Brimington, where he spoke to P.C. Wright about his daughter's disappearance. Gough had followed at a distance, and after a brief conversation with them he proceeded towards Chesterfield.

Before he reached the town, Alfred fell into the company of Thomas Holmes, also known as 'Mansfield Tom'. Holmes was to testify at Gough's trial that Gough had said to him,

> "We have met many times on this road, but we shall not meet again".

Holmes said,

> "What have you done wrong?",

to which Gough replied,

> "I will tell you when we meet again".

Gough continued into Chesterfield, where he left his cart at the shop of Thomas Newbury, a dealer who sometimes bought his rags. He lodged at the Beehive lodging house in Chesterfield that night.

Meanwhile, the disappearance of Eleanor had caused a stir. Charles Abney Brown, recollecting his discussion with Gough and Mr. Windle, set out the next morning to search for the girl. Brown noticed that the tracks of Gough's handcart led into Hooles Plantation, which lay off a semi-private road from Staveley to Barrow Hill. The first thing he saw was an onion bag and then, about twenty yards from this find, he came across the body of Eleanor Windle.

She had been raped, and then strangled with a strip of sacking. A piece of coloured wallpaper found nearby was later found to match that of a type in Gough's handcart. Gough was arrested and charged with murder.

For some reason, the trial took place at Leicester instead of Derby. The judge was Mr. Justice Matthews, the Crown was represented by the Hon. Chandos-Leigh, Q.C., and Mr. Etherington-Smith, while Gough employed the services of Mr. Weightman.

Weightman tried lamely to claim that the little girl might have been murdered by someone else, a passing collier perhaps. The jury were not impressed.

Gough's crime had aroused such revulsion in the minds of Derbyshire folk that nobody could be found willing to organise a campaign for his reprieve, so his execution was inevitable.

The *Reporter* did some research into Gough's character and past history while he was awaiting his end. Some interesting facts emerged. He had previously been a policeman with the Leeds Constabulary, and then a soldier in the 17th Foot, serving in India. Up to this point, Gough had led a respectable life, but he found it hard to adjust to civilian life on his return to this country.

He became an itinerant vendor, preferring to frequent lodging houses rather than seeking a more stable domestic existence.

The crime had aroused a great deal of interest. This was reflected in the size of the crowd that assembled outside the County Gaol in the pouring rain on 21st November 1881. Over one thousand people congregated to witness the tolling of the bell which symbolised the passing of life of Alfred Gough.